ADVANCE PRAISE

"Eric, my first boss, has written his story that centers on working hard and winning—the lessons that I first got from him at Morgan Stanley as a first-year associate are ones that I rely upon today."

—RUTH PORAT, SVP & CHIEF FINANCIAL
OFFICER, ALPHABET AND GOOGLE

"Eric Gleacher's memoir reads like a thrilling adventure story—full of perils and successes. It is engagingly written and contains valuable lessons about business, philanthropy, and life. Readers are in for an unusual treat!"

—MORTON SCHAPIRO, PROFESSOR AND
PRESIDENT, NORTHWESTERN UNIVERSITY

"In his new book, Eric Gleacher tells fascinating behind-the-scenes stories and shares his views about leadership and the value of philanthropy. Filled with entertaining and engaging stories about life in the Marines, mergers and acquisition,

and sports, *Risk. Reward. Repeat.* encourages people to take risks, reminds them to remember those who help along the way, and provides guidance for living an enriching and fulfilling life."

—ROBERT J. ZIMMER, PRESIDENT, UNIVERSITY OF CHICAGO

"There are no shortcuts in life to success. Reading Eric's memoir takes you on a wild journey showing what it takes to be successful in the world of business. A fascinating read where the qualities of honesty, hard work, and the importance of winning shine through."

—LUKE DONALD, PGA TOUR PLAYER AND FORMER NUMBER ONE RANKED GOLFER IN THE WORLD FOR FIFTY-SIX WEEKS

RISK. REWARD. REPEAT.

RISK. REWARD. REPEAT.

HOW I SUCCEEDED AND HOW YOU CAN TOO

ERIC GLEACHER

RISK. REWARD. REPEAT. RISK. REWARD. REPEAT. RISK. REWARD. REPEAT. RISK. REWARD. REPEAT.

JEG
P R E S S

RISK. REWARD. REPEAT.

How I Succeeded and How You Can Too

ISBN   978-1-5445-1922-7 *Hardcover*

978-1-5445-1921-0 *Paperback*

978-1-5445-1920-3 *Ebook*

978-1-5445-1961-6 *Audiobook*

This book is dedicated to all the Gleachers—six children, five spouses, stepson and spouse, and eight grandchildren—and especially to my lovely wife, Paula, who finds fun for us somewhere every day while keeping the train securely on the tracks.

CONTENTS

———

FOREWORD

———

ERIC GLEACHER IS A MAN WITH A COMPELLING STORY. HE has always been determined to excel in all that he attempts and has never failed to exceed the very high expectations he sets for himself. This autobiography reads like a novel. It is the story of a tournament-winning amateur golfer; an officer in the Marine Corps; an investment banker who became one of the half-dozen who dominated the M&A and takeover business that changed Wall Street and American business in the latter part of the last century; and a man who had the courage to leave a position as a senior partner at a famous and immensely successful investment bank to establish his own firm. I have known Eric for more than forty years—first as a lawyer he consulted with when he established the M&A department at Lehman Brothers, then almost immediately as a close friend. We and our families have been friends to this day. I'm the unique reader who was with Eric through most of what he recounts since we met. I've read the story twice. It's as stirring and interesting as when we lived it. You won't want to stop reading until the last page.

Martin Lipton
Wachtell, Lipton, Rosen & Katz

THE WORLD BELONGS TO THE AGGRESSIVE

———

I WALKED INTO THE NATIONAL AIRPORT TERMINAL OFF the flight from Chicago and immediately saw a man in military fatigues. I approached and stated my name. He told me to board a green bus outside the main exit and remain silent. The bus was almost full and completely quiet. We pulled out and drove to Quantico, VA. Not a sound during the thirty-six-mile trip. Quantico is the home of the FBI Academy and the Marine Corps' Training and Test Regiment. The name is certainly apropos for what the next thirteen weeks would hold for me and 319 other Marine officer candidates: some training and a lot of testing. We were assembled alphabetically and led to a squad bay where we were to sleep in bunk beds until graduation or expulsion from officer candidate school. Everyone was savvy enough not to break the silence, and we all knew the real "fun" would start in the morning.

The following morning we formed long lines. We started

our day with an array of unidentified inoculations shot into our right arms all at once by pistol-looking devices that had been designed for speed with no concern for pain experienced by the recipient. Next, we were marched to a large barbershop, where our heads were shaved. We were actually charged fifty cents for this "service," and believe me, there was no tipping. Next, all 320 candidates marched into an auditorium. A distinguished-looking older man (probably age forty-five or so) wearing a uniform with three stars on the epaulets and many medals on the left breast walked out onto the stage. The candidates were standing at rigid attention, and he did not offer to put us at ease. He welcomed us to Officer Candidate School (OCS) and told us he was in command of all USMC operations at Quantico. Then he dropped the hammer. He said, "Look to your left and look to your right—one of those two men will not be here when this officer candidate course is completed," and turned and walked off the stage. You may have seen something similar in the movies and think the general's remarks sound cliché. I can assure you that in 1963, every wide-eyed candidate standing at attention in that auditorium thought his words predicted a brutal experience to come at OCS.

The general's comments were the equivalent of a torpedo penetrating the side of a ship and exploding; no one knows at that instant whether the ship will sink or float. The odds of graduating from OCS had just been set at 50:50, making the chance of becoming a Marine officer a much riskier proposition than advertised by the recruiters who had signed up all 320 candidates. Believe me, the recruiters did not explain those odds.

There was no alternative. The officer candidates had volunteered because they wanted to earn the prestige of being a Marine officer for the rest of their lives. If one quit or was forced to leave OCS, one had to serve two years as a private and go through boot camp at Parris Island, SC with a bunch of seventeen-year-old high school drop-out recruits, carrying forever the stigma of one who could not cut it at OCS. I committed to myself to keep trying until death rather than conceding to the physical safety of failure. This attitude (I was 100 percent serious) would serve me well when the pressure was applied during training.

I survived the gauntlet of OCS with 159 other candidates, exactly half of the 320 who began the program. Each of the eight platoons, which started with forty candidates, graduated exactly twenty brand new 2d lieutenants! USMC officers do not lie to the troops, and in this instance, the odds quoted by the general were realized with military precision.

After six months at Officers Basic School at Quantico, I received orders to report to the 2d Marine Division at Camp Lejeune, NC. I drove down from Quantico and found a room in a BOQ (bachelor officer quarters). I had orders to report to G Company, 2d Battalion, Eighth Marines, and I found my way to its headquarters the next morning.

I arrived at G Company and learned the unit was out in the field training and would not return to company headquarters for a couple of days. I was a brand new second lieutenant rifle platoon leader, the classic starting job for Marine officers. The first sergeant was the only person at HQ and suggested I use the time to review the service records of the members of my platoon. He was very southern, had gray hair in a tight crew cut, and a slight potbelly. Time would prove him to be the indispensable member of G Company. Each platoon had three rifle squads, each headed by a sergeant, and a weapons platoon carrying machine guns and other weapons more lethal than the M14s the riflemen in the rifle squads carried.

I do not recall a single class at OCS or Officers Basic School about leadership. I think the Marine Corps is comfortable dealing in facts, military tactics, and weapons. How to be a leader of men doesn't fit comfortably in that format. There are plenty of stories of troops shooting incompetent lieutenants in the back in combat situations, allowing experienced sergeants to take command and save the platoon from disastrous consequences. So, if you are a twenty-three-year-old second lieutenant, green as green can be, poised to take command of an experienced rifle platoon, you best figure out your situation quickly.

The first folder I chose was Staff Sergeant James Dixon's, my platoon sergeant. He was a square-jawed, somewhat grizzled Northern Californian who was parsimonious with his words. He was an incredibly competent infantry Marine. Sergeant Dixon had fought in the Korean War, where he established a distinguished combat record. Later, he had an altercation in a noncommissioned officers club, which escalated dangerously. Sergeant Dixon attacked his adversary with an ice pick and fortunately did not kill him. He was court-martialed and demoted to private but was not sent to prison, probably because of his meritorious combat record. He had worked himself back up to staff sergeant, and in a couple of days, I would become his "superior officer!" Winning Sergeant Dixon's respect seemed even more intimidating than the general saying, "Look to the left...look to the right." Moreover, half of the platoon's troops had been deployed in the Cuban Missile Crisis a year earlier, poised aboard a ship offshore to make an amphibious landing, and were highly trained infantry Marines. I was sure they did not suffer fools!

Over time, James Dixon and I became friends, albeit with a respectful amount of distance between us, as was appropriate between officers and enlisted men. He always called me lieutenant, never Eric, and almost never Lieutenant Gleacher, just lieutenant. I always referred to him as Sergeant Dixon, "Sarndixen" pronounced as a single word, and I never once called him James. When we were deployed in Panama, we would sleep side-by-side on our air mattresses outside on the Cristobal Pier after many Heinekens, twenty-five cents a bottle in the Canal Zone. Sarndixen would tell me stories about his experiences in the historic Chosin Reservoir Campaign in North Korea, legendary in the annals of Marine Corps history, until one of us fell asleep.

Making my way through OCS, taking charge of the platoon of forty-five men, and earning their respect as well as James Dixon's, had an immensely positive effect on my self-image, self-confidence, and future behavior. I learned I had to be myself; there was no other choice. I learned flawless integrity was a must, no space for anything less. I learned the pursuit of excellence was a critical attitude in any endeavor. I learned there were plenty of smart, capable people of all shapes and colors—many of whom never finished high school—who one could influence and motivate and who could achieve amazing results. I learned to delegate and trust and discovered that most of the time, people exceed expectations. All this from a standing start wondering if James Dixon could ever accept me as his superior officer. This was part of what being a Marine infantry officer would give back to me, affecting the rest of my life. And all of these experiences proved to be as applicable in business as they were in the USMC.

Of all the lessons of leadership learned in the Marines, perhaps the most impactful was not to ask anyone to do something you couldn't do as well or better—leading by example. In weapons qualification, I went from being an average marksman to shooting high expert with both the M14 and 45-caliber pistol. I am absolutely convinced the improvement was due to my motivation to score higher than anyone else in my platoon. I carried over that philosophy into my business career, and it served me well. I wanted to know as much about accounting as the CFO, so I wasn't vulnerable to negative surprises or dishonesty in the process of working on a merger or securities offering. If we were working on a deal, it was not unusual for the team to have so much to do that the workday would stretch well into the night. Sometimes we would work until 4 am for a week or more. I made sure I was the last to leave and the first one back in the office the following morning. And I never lost motivation on my most serious, privately kept quest: to be regarded as the best in the world at mergers and acquisitions (M&A). The will to win is a powerful force if one can harness it.

My decision to volunteer for service in the Marine Corps rather than one of the six-month reserve programs readily available at the time proved brilliant. That decision was straightforward for me. I wanted the toughest possible challenge, not the easy way out. The confidence I gained from this experience was more valuable and important to the way I conducted myself in future years than anything else I had ever done. Finally, I had earned a positive self-image, a critical factor that had been previously absent. The world belongs to the aggressive. Don't underestimate that assertion.

THE EARLY YEARS

———

I WAS TWELVE YEARS OLD, LIVING IN BLAIR, NE, A SMALL town along the Missouri River north of Omaha. We moved quite often to wherever my father found work: Barranquilla, Colombia; Fresno, California; and Kansas City, Missouri, were previous stopovers. One day, a shipment arrived from our prior location, which included a set of ladies' golf clubs. Little did I know these golf clubs would influence where I went to college, how I landed my first job, the establishment of many meaningful relationships, and even love interests.

My father, Joseph George Gleacher, was born on October 26, 1904, in Mount Vernon, NY. His mother died at age twenty-four, less than a year after his birth, and he was raised by his father, Joseph Patrick Gleacher, and an aunt in Bridgeport, CT. His father was a tinsmith. When my father was eighteen and still in high school, he became a professional boxer. He fought under the name Joe Morgan, pseudonymity being a common practice those days as boxing suffered from stigma and was illegal in certain states. He was successful and became the bantamweight (126-pound) professional champion of Connecticut. He lost very few bouts and received much publicity in the Bridgeport press—they called him "The Schoolboy Champion." Unfortunately, he lost a tooth, which cost him admission to the Coast Guard Academy when he graduated from high school. There was no money for regular college tuition, so he worked in construction, eventually qualifying as a construction engineer—a civil engineer without a college degree.

After the attack on Pearl Harbor, my father joined the Seabees. I was one and a half years old (born April 27, 1940). The Seabees are the US Naval Construction Battalions responsible for militarized construction projects. I don't know everything he did during the war, but I know my father spent most of his time in the Marianas Islands— Guam, Tinian, and Saipan. Tinian is the least populous of the larger islands of the Marianas, and the Seabees constructed airfields there, which enabled the bombers to be armed and launched toward Japan where they would drop their payloads and return without having to refuel. Tinian was extremely strategic, and the combat there was intense. The Marines and Seabees were constantly under attack by the Japanese, but somehow they managed to build and defend their airfields and related facilities. The destruction their bombers wreaked on the Japanese mainland ended the war with Japan. The Germans had already surrendered in Europe, and World War II was over.

I tried to talk to my father about his experiences in the war many times over the years. He never once was willing. I do know that at the war's end, he was a battalion commander, and he remained in the Naval Reserve for twenty years thereafter.

My mother, Marjory Carr Gleacher, was born on December 21, 1903, in Lawrence, MA. She and I stayed in Florida during the war. We were alone and knew no one. My mother was unusual. I never knew her to have a friend, not even one. I never met anyone from her family except her mother, who spoke very little English. My mother did not drive a car. She took care of our living space and cooked. That was it.

Late one night, when I was four years old, she had a lengthy argument with our landlord in Florida. She complained that something was wrong with our apartment, but even my four-year-old brain realized her claim was absurd. The landlord finally had enough and threatened to evict us right then and there, and it seemed like we were about to be out on the street with no place to go. I was stunned by my mother's lack of judgment, and I remember being terrified. Somehow the ridiculous argument ended, and we were not evicted, but the trauma I experienced shook me to my core. I realized from that point on I would have to be alert and look out for myself. That mindset has never changed.

GROWING UP

―――

ONE AFTERNOON, MY DAD AND I WENT TO A NINE-HOLE golf course near Blair, NE. I was immediately able to whack the ball and get around the course without a problem. I am pretty sure my dad was impressed, although he was not one to heap praise indiscriminately. I don't remember if I shot a score, but I remember the golf course. The fee to play was fifty cents left in a wooden box on a bench near the first tee. The course had sand greens, and if you missed a fairway, your ball was gone, as tall cornfields lined every hole. Once on the green, you drew a line in the sand from your ball to the hole before putting. I liked the whole experience. I was out with my dad, and I learned I could be good at golf.

After a few months, my dad completed his work on the Missouri River and found another job in Norfolk, VA. We remained in Norfolk for two and a half years, which was the longest we ever stayed in one place. My dad continued in the Naval Reserve after the war and was eligible to join the Officers' Golf Club in Norfolk, which was far superior to the sand greens course in Nebraska. It was called the Sewells Point Golf Club. I started working on golf as my primary sport. This was in March of 1953, a month before my thirteenth birthday. I improved rapidly. I took two buses every day after school to reach Sewells Point. I played my first tournament in June and won a beautiful sterling silver cup (which I still have), shooting 79 at the Princess Anne Country Club in Virginia Beach. The tournament, which was for boys thirteen and under, was called the McClanan Invitational in honor of Billy McClanan, who died too early in his life.

That was it! Golf was my game, and I was going to give it my all to become a great player. John O'Donnell was the pro at Sewells Point and was one of the best players in Virginia. He had a son my age, and Johnny and I played together all the time. Mr. O'Donnell took an interest in me and became my first professional coach. A month after winning the McClanan trophy, I went on my first trip without parental supervision. Bill Dudley, the sixteen-year-old son of a Navy Admiral, and I took a 280-mile train ride to Roanoke to play in the Virginia State Junior Championship at the Hidden Valley Country Club. Bill and I shared a room in the Ponce de Leon Hotel and took a taxi back and forth from the course every day. We never had a problem during our stay, and I won the thirteen and under championship, defeating Charlie Holden in the final match. I won a clock engraved with the tournament details, which has not survived the years. What has survived is my friendship with Charlie Holden, which continues to this day. Charlie grew up in Alexandria, VA where he took over the family insurance business upon his father's retirement. Charlie is five days older than I am, and when we turned fifty, we played a rematch at the Pine Valley Golf Club in NJ. Again, I prevailed.

I attended ten different schools across the US plus a year in South America. Many wanted me to advance a grade, sometimes two, but fortunately, my father had good judgment and did not allow it to happen. I became very independent as a result of this nomadic existence but also missed out on many aspects of childhood most people take for granted. No tears, as I learned to always look forward, not back at the past.

North Plainfield, NJ, our next destination, proved to be a brief stop along the progression of many such stops. I played for the high school golf team but have no lasting memories of time spent there. After my father's stint in North Plainfield, he had to find another job. This was not the only time he finished one job without immediately having another. There never was any significant money available as a cushion, so those periods were stressful and made a lasting and deep impression on me.

We moved once again to my grandfather's home in Bridgeport—a houseboat on land with a dock out into Ash Creek—which flowed in and out of Long Island Sound. My dad eventually found a job as a consulting engineer on a section of Interstate 95, which was under construction along the East Coast. The company he joined was responsible for inspecting and approving the work of the contractors building the highway.

We rented a house in Fairfield, CT (we never owned our own home), and I attended Roger Ludlowe High School. The school was overcrowded, and students either attended the morning or afternoon session. I went in the afternoon. Once again, I had to start over and make new friends. Being on the golf team was a big help, but sophomore year in high school required other skills and sophistication, which I lacked. I was socially awkward and had some fringe relationships with people who were not particularly desirable. Fortunately, I never had any serious problems, but I was certainly too close to the line.

It took well into my college years to catch up socially to where I was intellectually and athletically. Growing up, I never considered myself a leader. I was far from being the class president, a member of the student council, or editor of the newspaper. In fact, other than being a talented junior golfer, my self-image and self-esteem were decidedly lackluster, most likely in the bottom quartile for people my age. Money was always tight and a constant source of concern. I had no long-term friends and little knowledge or comfort with social graces. I never had a girlfriend until I went to college.

My golfing performance continued to improve. We won the state high school championship at Ludlowe and were runners-up at Andrew Warde High School, where I transferred in my junior year. I won most of the junior championships around New York and Connecticut, including the Connecticut Jaycee Junior, the Metropolitan Golf Association match play, and New York Journal-American medal play titles. In the USGA National Junior Championship, I lost in the third round to the eventual champion and did well in all the other national junior competitions.

My academic performance correlated with my lack of balance in social relationships. I had a 2.5 grade point average and rarely opened a book in high school. This was not helpful when applying to college but was counterbalanced by my competitive golf résumé and respectable SAT scores. I was accepted to the University of Pennsylvania—much to the chagrin of many of my classmates—who had persevered throughout high school and been rejected. In the yearbook, I was depicted as the class clown, something I have been embarrassed about since. But I must admit it was an accurate reflection of my attitude and lack of sophistication during my high school years. In college, I was more mature and diligent, but it was my time in the Marines that shaped my values, moral compass, and self-confidence, giving me the ability to pursue a successful life and career.

In June 1958, I graduated from high school, and later that

day, my mother, father, and I got into our car and headed to Chicago. My father had a new job as head maintenance engineer for the highway system in Illinois. This was a good job, one he held until he retired many years later.

We moved into a garden apartment in Skokie, a north-side suburb. Once again, I was in a new place and didn't know a soul. So I did the one thing I did best: I competed in golf tournaments. I played in the Cook County Amateur at Columbus Park, the Chicago Amateur at Jackson Park, and the Midwest Amateur at Waveland Park, located along Lake Michigan, adjacent to the Outer Drive. I defeated some of the top players in Chicago and reached the semifinals of the Cook County Amateur. People had no clue who I was, and some were curious. Harry Mussatto, the golf coach at Western Illinois University, asked about my college plans. I told him I was accepted at the University of Pennsylvania in the Ivy League, and I was going to go there. He said he had an outstanding golf program at Western Illinois and invited me to visit the campus so he could show me around. I said thank you, but I am going to Penn, and my mind is made up. I played in the tournaments and did well, but I was deluding myself about ever being a student at Penn.

My high school GPA was marginal, so Penn offered a full scholarship if I got a C average or better in the first semester. Sounded like a no-brainer; how could I say no? It was such a prestigious part of my almost nonexistent self-image that

I couldn't give up and admit I was not going to get to Penn. The fact was there was no money. How could I survive the first semester, much less pay the tuition? Had I been more clever, I would have gotten on a bus, showed up at Penn, tried to get a loan, and somehow figured things out and powered forward. But I didn't.

I hung on to the dream until the tournament golf season ended and reality hit. My father got me a job working as a laborer on a segment of the Illinois Toll Road, which was under construction. I drove paving stakes with a sledgehammer which allowed the engineers to mark the elevations and set the forms to pour concrete for the road surface. I worked seven days a week, all day, every day because the technology to pour concrete in temperatures under thirty-two degrees did not yet exist, so everything stopped when the mercury dipped below freezing. It was a race against the weather. I worked from the end of August until the end of November. I didn't have a day off for three months, and the work provided excellent physical conditioning. The job paid well, and I enjoyed working with the unique assortment of people who followed the construction trades around the country. However, I was not going anywhere, and when the cold weather hit and the work ended, I had nothing to do. I decided it was time to visit Harry Mussatto at Western Illinois University.

WESTERN ILLINOIS UNIVERSITY

MY FATHER DROVE US DOWN TO CAMPUS, AND WE HAD a nice day with Harry. I decided to take his offer. I got a full-tuition scholarship, which was $40 a quarter! Western was a State Teachers College in Macomb, IL, 200 miles south of Chicago. I was told I would have to major in physical education coaching. Why would I do that? Because when golf season started in the spring, Harry wanted to ensure my eligibility, and no athlete majoring in PE ever received a failing grade. And so that's what I did. They gave me a field house job, which I never actually had to do. It was a way for the athletic department to put a few dollars in my pocket.

Spring arrived, and we started the golf season. We made a trip through Tennessee, Georgia, and Florida, playing matches against the best teams in the country—University of Florida, Florida State, Auburn, and others. I averaged 72 for the ten matches we played and solidified my position as the number two man on the team. I was eighteen, and the rest of the players were in their early twenties. Most had spent a few years in the military, but because I was a good player, they harassed me less than an eighteen-year-old might expect.

I had a great roommate, Bill Brick, who had just been discharged from the Army and had come to Western to play golf. We got along extremely well and lived in a rooming house for student residents. We did our homework and went out for dinner every night, and had a good time on the weekends. Life was good.

We played thirty matches that spring, won our conference championship, and then played in the NAIA national championship. The National Association of Intercollegiate Athletics was (and still is) the NCAA for small colleges, a big deal as there were hundreds of small colleges and universities in the US. The tournament was at Quincy Country Club in Quincy, IL and our number one player, Jim King, won the individual championship, and our team won the team championship. We became national champions forever.

I went back to Chicago that summer, played in the park district tournaments again, and had an even better season than I had the year before. I won the Cook County Amateur, was runner-up in the Chicago Amateur, and finished in the top five in the Midwest Amateur. I went back to Western Illinois in the fall.

I transferred into a liberal arts program because I realized I could get A's in any course in which I did the homework and attended all the classes. Winter arrived—which is unrelenting 200 miles south of Chicago in the prairies where the wind howls and the temperatures get very cold. I began to regret never figuring out how to get myself to Penn, and the belief I should be going to a top school returned. Western was fun, I discovered girls, and the golf was outstanding, but there was one big thing missing: what was I going to do with my life? If I stayed at Western, I was almost certainly going to be a golf pro, and I knew from my experience in national level competition I was good, but others were better, such as Jack Nicklaus. In those days, there was money in professional golf if you were Jack or Arnold Palmer or Gary Player. Beyond those stars, it wasn't attractive financially.

I decided I wanted to get into a top university and the nearest one I could identify was Northwestern. Also, my parents lived in Skokie, which was close to Evanston, where Northwestern is located. I figured if I could get admitted to Northwestern, I would be able to do the work, as I had learned how to apply myself and study effectively. The golf coach at Northwestern was Sid Richardson, who was the ticket manager at Dyche Stadium, where the football team played. I went home for the weekend, and that Monday, I went to the ticket office at the stadium. I had no appointment because I didn't know about making appointments. I asked for Sid Richardson, and fortunately, he was there. I told him I wanted to go to a top school and would be interested in transferring to Northwestern. He knew all about me because he followed Chicago golf in the newspapers and had me admitted in three days! Then the hard part began.

I borrowed my father's car and drove back to Western. I told Coach Mussatto I was transferring to Northwestern, thinking he would understand. Not even close! He said it made no sense, Western was a great school, I could get just as good an education there as I could at Northwestern, and Western had a far superior golf program. He took me to see the president of the university and a couple of professors, and my head was spinning. I was nineteen years old and didn't know what to think. Harry was the first adult with whom I had established a close relationship other than my father, and I was really confused about what to do. Finally, I concluded I couldn't go against Coach Mussatto and would stay at Western.

I asked a friend from the golf team, Pat McElwee, to keep me company while driving up to Chicago to drop off my father's car. We would be able to catch a train back to Macomb. Pat said yes, and we stopped on the way out of town to have a couple of beers at the Pace Hotel bar. We finally drove out of town, and all of a sudden, Pat said, "Pull this car over. This is crazy! You get a chance to go to Northwestern, where they are going to give you a scholarship to play golf, and you are talking about staying at Western Illinois. Turn this car around. We're going back to your room to pack your stuff, and you're getting the hell out of here." That is exactly what he said and exactly what we did. We went back to my room, packed everything up, and drove to Skokie at one o'clock in the morning. Without that bit of fortitude acquired at the Pace bar combined with the unemotional sensibility of Pat McElwee, my life certainly would have turned out differently.

I never said goodbye to Harry Mussatto, which I was embarrassed about for many years. Harry provided an important adult influence when I was eighteen to nineteen years old. Looking back, I see how significant his presence was. He was with me all summer when I was competing in the tournaments. He would take me out to dinner, give me advice about my next match, encourage me, and build me up. He was a leader, a role model, and an adult friend. To have an accomplished person of high integrity as a mentor, particularly given my unusual background, is something I am grateful for to this day. Harry died before I ever squared things up with him, but later in my life, I found a way to pay tribute to him. Western had a 9-hole golf course, as did most of the small towns in central Illinois. I came up with the idea and money to build a second nine, thus creating an 18-hole course. The university made the land available, and we hired the same architects who built the original nine.

Having an 18-hole course added prestige and enhanced the recruitment of men and women college golfers at Western while also providing an improved recreational facility for local residents. When the work was completed, I flew to Macomb to dedicate the course. I am told that my Falcon 900 was the largest plane ever to land at the tiny Macomb airport! My old teammates—Al Barkow, a well-known golf writer, and Emil Esposito, a top golf pro in Chicago—came for the dedication. The three of us played golf and hung out for two days beforehand. It was as if we had picked up right where we left off during our time together at Western. So much fun! At the ceremony in front of a large crowd, we unveiled a statue of Harry and announced the golf course had been named the Harry Mussatto Golf Course. Harry's wife and three daughters were there, as was my roommate Bill Brick's widow and their daughter. To say this was an emotional experience would be a major understatement. I will never forget it.

NORTHWESTERN UNIVERSITY

A FEW DAYS AFTER LEAVING WESTERN, I STARTED classes at Northwestern. The kids were sharp and even looked a bit different—hard to explain. The campus was beautiful, and it all felt otherworldly. Since I was a student-athlete who had transferred from another school, I was required by NCAA rules to sit out for a year before I could compete. I would become eligible in time for the 1961 season when my scholarship would start. My father worked a second job at night at a golf driving range to earn the money for my tuition during that interim period, which I have never forgotten.

I was allowed to practice with the team even though I was ineligible to compete. I became friendly with the guys and really hit it off with Gary Levering, a junior from Kansas City. We became immediate friends, and Gary invited me to join his fraternity, Delta Upsilon. This turned out to be a major step forward as 80 percent of the students at Northwestern were "Greeks," members of sororities and fraternities. For those outside the Greek system, social life was complicated. The fraternities and sororities had relationships and had parties together, which facilitated social interaction between men and women. I am certain had I not met Gary, life at Northwestern as a commuter would have been very different.

I eventually lived in the DU house, made many friends, and enjoyed some spectacular roommates, including Paul Flatley, an All-American flanker back who went on to become rookie of the year in the NFL with the Vikings, and Jay Robertson, a life-long friend and fellow Marine who served in Vietnam. Jay was a walk-on football player who became sole captain of the team in his senior year, an amazing accomplishment in Big Ten football. There were many exceptional DUs, and I soaked up the environment. Gary and I remained good friends until he passed a few years ago. We played golf, did things with our kids, and made investments together. Gary and I and a few other partners bought a building in Houston where Bush 41 established his office when he retired from public life.

My devotion to golf did not wane even though the team, the program, and the coach were substandard compared to Western Illinois. Sid Richardson had a negative personality and deflated the players, unlike Harry Mussatto, who was upbeat and positive. Gary and I resolved that if we were successful in our lives, we would offer NU significant financial support in exchange for retiring Sid. He died long before we were in a position to do so.

I played number one for the two years of my eligibility and was co-captain of the team senior year with Ed Menke, a scrappy, scrambling player who unfortunately died of leukemia the summer after graduation. What a loss.

We had a weak team and a lousy coach those two years, but all the players made the best of it, and I personally vowed to make it better in the future if I could. I had seen the template with Harry Mussatto at Western. If it could work there, it could work at Northwestern.

When I arrived at Northwestern, I was intimidated. People at Western Illinois assumed students at NU were geniuses. After attending some classes, I realized I was just as smart as anyone else walking the halls. I majored in American History. The lectures and reading were interesting and enjoyable. I had a respectable 3.3 GPA, tried as hard as I could on the golf course, and added another element to my life: social activity!

I became well known in the Kappa Kappa Gamma house, which was loaded with attractive, intelligent girls. I met a very special one, Susan Griffith, from East Grand Rapids, MI. She was eighteen and I was twenty, and almost immediately, we stopped dating anyone else. By today's standards, we were incredibly young to do so, but it was not unusual at the time. Susan was the youngest of three sisters; her dad was an OB/GYN and her mom an elegant lady who lived to 102 years of age. I attended her 100th birthday party, and she still had all circuits firing. I loved hitchhiking up to Grand Rapids and hanging out with Susan and her mom and dad. I had never known a family environment like theirs, and it was a wonderful new experience. Susan and I married when she graduated in 1964, and we had three children: John (October 25, 1966), Sarah (November 9, 1968), and James (September 26, 1970). Susan taught school at Camp Lejeune while I served in the Marines. We saved the money she earned and lived off my USMC compensation. When I was discharged, we were able to buy a new car and pay my initial tuition at The University of Chicago Graduate School of Business with her earnings. After a couple of terms, I was awarded a Fellowship and worked part-time as a counselor at the business school's evening program. I also received the GI Bill, which was a godsend. Many years later, I established a veterans' scholarship program at the school to help veterans close the gap between the GI Bill and the total costs of attending full-time. Susan was a wonderful partner and mother to our three young children. Unfortunately, we divorced in 1978 but feel we accomplished a lot together and get along well today.

I lost quite a few course credits from Western and had to attend summer school and fall quarter in order to graduate in December 1962. I was admitted to Northwestern Law School starting in February 1963, even though I knew nothing about what a law career entailed. Susan would not graduate for two years, and we figured I could complete two years of law school and keep my student deferment from the draft. The old adage "all good things come to an end" arose when I received a letter from the law school stating their 100-year-old practice of having a mid-year entering class had been terminated and all new classes would now start in September. This meant I would be drafted into the military before I could start law school because my student deferment would expire when I graduated. I had no idea when my draft notice would arrive, so I decided to find a job. I did not know how to look for one, so I put on a suit and walked into the American National Bank on LaSalle Street in Chicago and announced to the doorman I had just graduated from Northwestern University and wanted to talk to someone about a job. Surprisingly, he called HR, and they said to send me up! I was interviewed and offered a job on the spot. Once again, so much for making appointments!

I was assigned to the Industrial Department of the bank. The name was a misnomer because, as far as I could determine, the only industry the department engaged in was floor planning auto loans for the huge Chicago car dealers. The dealers were so large and sold so many cars, their auto loan business was extremely lucrative for the banks. In an effort to secure business, banks would agree to finance virtually any customer with a driver's license and a job. This was called floor planning. Obviously, there would be some bad loans but spread among hundreds of good loans, the losses were tolerable. Also, there was a mechanism that further mitigated the bad loans: repossession of the vehicles.

My job was to call the delinquent owners after they were two months behind on their payments and inform them their car would be repossessed by the bank if they did not make a payment. Most of the calls were highly spirited and profane. My only duty at the bank was to make these calls from nine to five every day.

There was a separate crew who repossessed the vehicles. This was extremely dangerous work. They never came to the bank during the day because their job was conducted at night. Once in a while, they made house calls in the afternoon and took me along, but they refused to take me at night. When someone actually opened a door, which was not often, the conversation was not social. I'm not sure the afternoon visits accomplished anything, but they solidified my belief that I was going to find a better way to make a living.

There was another lesson learned during my two months at the American National Bank. After a few weeks, I realized a number of recent college graduates were participants in a management training program. All were working toward getting their MBAs from various evening programs in Chicago. I had not been invited to join this group, which made me feel like a second-class citizen. Of course, people in the group had most likely been recruited the spring before graduation, and I had walked in off the street and solicited the doorman in January. Nevertheless, I was determined not to find myself in a similar position again and to get my MBA as soon as I'd completed my service obligation and before I found a job. It was clear an MBA differentiated one from those who had only undergraduate degrees.

My draft notice arrived, and I decided to volunteer for the Marines. I was not interested in taking the easy way out by signing up for one of the many six-month reserve programs available at the time. If I was going to serve, I wanted to accept the most challenging option available, and that was the Marines. I was sure the experience would be unlike any I might have in my future. My father was a combat veteran and wasn't concerned about me joining the Marine Corps. He was worried I would never go back to school and continue my education. I told him I would.

US MARINE CORPS (1963–1966)

I ARRIVED AT QUANTICO, AND ON THE FIRST DAY, HAD my head shaved and my body inoculated by pistol injection. I received heartfelt greetings from a general who announced the odds of becoming a Marine officer were 50:50. During the second day at Quantico, as if matters weren't sufficiently complicated, I managed to slip in a wet stairwell and injure my right shoulder when I grabbed the banister to avoid falling. The drill instructor was running the platoon up and down the stairs during a lull between activities, and there was light snow on the ground, which made the stairs slippery. The following morning I could hardly move my arm. Fortunately, it loosened up during the day, and I was able to function as if it hadn't happened. I kept it to myself and ignored the pain when I did something that made it hurt. Years later, I required surgery as the joint had loosened, and my shoulder would occasionally work its way out of its socket in my sleep.

OCS was difficult but manageable, with the right mix of athleticism, endurance, and attitude. For example, many athletic requirements, such as the obstacle course, forced marches over the steep Hill Trail, and running around the grinder after an exhausting hike were designed to determine who would quit and who wouldn't and who really wanted to be a Marine officer. The drill instructors wanted to see who would continue when the lactic acid was making legs cramp and scream. One had to really want to succeed to not be vulnerable when these short-term physical crises emerged. I was fortunate. I was not able to easily do pull-ups because of my shoulder problem, but I could do enough that my fitness as a potential officer was not questioned. On the other hand, my endurance was as good as or better than anyone else's in my platoon. The toughest forced march, the most grueling, seemingly unending run never gave me a problem. Others did not fare as well. The big ex-football players had the most trouble with the physical and aerobic challenges of the endurance-oriented forced marches. They had substantial bodyweight to carry and seventy pounds of gear on their backs. Old athletic injuries often presented themselves on the trail. Our forty-man platoon got smaller every week.

The mental aspect of training was challenging, as well. The DIs were masters at sensing weakness or sensitivity and would hone in mercilessly on anyone who showed the signs. Some couldn't take the harassment and pressure the DIs applied. My solution was to regard the hazing as a game.

Anything they did to challenge me was simply an attempt to make me flinch. I played along and never reacted, thus denying the DIs a foothold to keep going. Others did react, and some left or were terminated from the program. There wasn't much military training at OCS. We learned to read a map and use a compass, and I recall a few exams but can't remember what they covered. The main focus was on who could handle the pressure and who would never quit—in short, who would be the best leaders in a combat situation.

OCS began with 320 candidates divided into eight platoons of forty men. At graduation, eight platoons of twenty men received their commissions as second lieutenants in the US Marine Corps. Exactly 50 percent were either privates down at Parris Island or had been medically discharged. I was so happy to have those little gold bars on my collar. My achievement gave me a rush of self-confidence more powerful than anything I'd ever imagined. My fiancé Susan and my parents were at Quantico to share it with me.

OCS graduation was on a Saturday. On Monday, the 160 newly minted second lieutenants began a six-month course at Quantico training to become Marine officers. Officers Basic School was very different from OCS. Physical training was ever-present, but the instructors were no longer pushing us to the limit to see who would give up. It was just good, hard PT, a constant activity in the Marines. We were divided alphabetically into four-man "suites," each with one bathroom—luxury compared to a forty-man squad bay with communal showers. Basic School was more academic, with courses in military tactics and history, analysis of legendary battles, and six weeks devoted to weapons. We moved out to the rifle range, put up our tents, and spent three weeks learning how to turn our M14 rifles and 45-caliber pistols into killing machines. We learned to take them apart, clean and oil all the pieces, and put them back together while blindfolded so in a combat situation, we could keep them operative under any conditions. We received scores on the rifle and pistol ranges, which indicated our competence with the weapons. At Basic School, I shot marksman with the M14 and the 45, the lowest acceptable qualifying score. The following year, when I was a rifle platoon commander in the Fleet Marine Force, spurred on by personal pride and ferocious desire to shoot a higher score than any of the forty-five men in my platoon, I qualified as a high expert with both weapons and realized my goal.

Basic School was like having a job. We had the freedom to go out at night (except when out in the field) and had weekends off. There was a women's college down the road in Fredericksburg called Mary Washington, which was extremely popular with the lieutenants. Half the girls would have nothing to do with the Marines, and the other half couldn't get enough of them! Susan and I had recently become engaged, so I missed out, except vicariously, on that whole scene. My three suitemates did not.

Toward the end of Basic School, each officer petitioned for the MOS[1] he wanted as well as his second and third choices. Infantry was the most sought after MOS because it was the "real" Marine Corps, and one sent there would become a rifle platoon commander, which was considered the heartbeat of the corps. Those selected as 0302's (infantry) were chosen based on their rank in the class (everyone was continually ranked based on test scores and general performance) and the qualitative assessment of the various instructors, most of whom were senior officers. I requested 0302 and was selected. We had a graduation gathering in the auditorium, followed by lunch in the cafeteria. Very military. Afterward, people said their goodbyes and drove down the road to begin real life in the US Marine Corps.

G Company and our battalion were either deployed or sent to train in the field at Camp Lejeune. Susan taught school on the base, and I was home once in a while. Within a month of my arrival at Lejeune, G-2-8 Marines were deployed to the Panama Canal zone because of communist-inspired riots that had resulted in twenty-three American deaths. Our battalion and a squadron of helicopters were loaded on LPH-7[2], the Guadalcanal, the first landing platform helicopter (LPH) ship to enter service. It was 500 feet long, about half the

---

1   Military Occupational Specialty code used to identify specific jobs.

2   A Landing Platform Helicopter naval ship 500 feet long transporting a squadron of Marine helicopters and a battalion of Marine infantry.

length of an aircraft carrier, and its primary function was to rapidly deploy Marine infantry into jungle or other terrain.

We spent four months in Panama on the Caribbean side of the isthmus. Panama City, on the other side, was on the Pacific Ocean. There were no riots while we were there. Our presence was a show of force: a big ship with lots of Marines and firepower. I completed the Army Jungle Warfare School at Coco Solo. We lived on boa constrictor (tastes like chicken) and fruit growing in the jungle. At night the jungle was pitch black because of the dense upper canopy, like being in a closet with the door closed. We learned which fruit was poisonous and which could be eaten. It was tricky business since most of the natural growth looks delicious when one is famished!

Panama worked well for me because I was with my platoon almost every day for four months, and by the time we returned to Lejeune, I had established myself as the platoon leader. On the way back to the US, we stopped at Guantanamo Bay, Cuba, for some liberty, which had not been available during the four months in Panama. This turned out to be a questionable move since the Marine officers fought the Navy officers after copious alcohol consumption, as did the Marine and Navy enlisted men. Too much booze ignited the fires of the usual interservice rivalries.

A month or so later, we were sent to the Little Creek, VA

amphibious warfare base to train naval academy midshipmen in amphibious landings. We lived aboard ship for six weeks and taught the middies how to hit the beach in mock combat situations.

After a month or so back at Lejeune, we began Operation Steelpike, a major joint training exercise with NATO conducted in Spain. Once again, we boarded LPH-7 and set sail with a large fleet of ships across the Atlantic. It took ten days to make the crossing, and the trip was not without drama. Unfortunately, a major helicopter collision happened out over the ocean, killing eleven people. After Steelpike, we sailed to Southport, England, and spent a few days with the Royal Marines, a really impressive force. We had some liberty and then returned to Lejeune. We were gone for more than a month.

I spent the remainder of 1964 training at Lejeune. Toward the end of the year, the arm I injured at OCS began to come out of its socket in my sleep. I had it surgically repaired at the naval hospital at Lejeune in early January 1965. My doctor asked if I wanted to apply for a medical discharge, and I said no. I wanted to finish the military career I signed up for.

My arm was bound to my chest for three weeks. When the wrapping was removed, I could barely lift my arm off my chest, but everyday exercise increased my mobility. After two weeks, I asked my doctor if I could play golf. I was on light duty and had nothing else to do. He said go ahead, but do not stress the arm. The first time I played, I shot 119. I couldn't get the club back very far, but each succeeding day I achieved more mobility. Late in April, three and a half months post-surgery, I won an interservice golf championship at Parris Island against 250 competitors from all branches of the military.

I was released from active duty with fifteen other lieutenants in May 1966. I had scored well on the exam required to apply to business school and gained admission to The University of Chicago's Graduate School of Business beginning in June. I was the only lieutenant going back to school, and the others thought I was crazy since jobs were easy to find, and almost all of us were married, some with children. My wife Susan was pregnant. But returning to school turned out to be one of the best and most important decisions of my life.

THE UNIVERSITY OF CHICAGO GRADUATE SCHOOL OF BUSINESS

AT THE END OF MAY 1966, SUSAN AND I GOT INTO OUR brand-new Chevrolet Malibu (it cost $2,750) and drove to East Grand Rapids, MI. We spent a week or so with Susan's parents and then continued on to Chicago. We arrived at The University of Chicago on a quiet summer evening. The campus was deserted. We had rented an apartment through the mail from student housing and did not have a key. We located the Graduate School of Business building and, fortunately, there was one light on at the very end of a corridor. We walked down the hall and found a man seated at a desk. There was one picture on the wall of his office, and it was of General Jonathan Wainwright, a famous Marine medal of honor recipient, who fought in the Pacific in the Second World War. I took this as a positive omen since the odds of the first person I would meet on The University of Chicago campus having a portrait of a Marine on his office wall had to be zero! The man behind the desk was Jeff Metcalf, the dean of students, himself a former Marine. We talked about the coincidence and other things. He arranged to have someone retrieve the key to our apartment, enabling us to stay there that night. I told Dean Metcalf I was nervous about starting at a school with such a reputation for difficulty. He told me, "Don't worry about it, I'm going to take care of you, and you're going to do great."

Well, he was correct in all respects. I was nervous at first, but from the beginning of my second quarter until graduation, I got mostly As. I loved all aspects of being at The University of Chicago. I learned about finance, marketing, and many other elements of business. It became clear to me finance was my area of interest. The University of Chicago provided the direction that guided me for my entire forty-five-year career.

I was in a hurry. Susan gave birth to John on October 25, 1966 at the Lying-in Hospital at The University of Chicago. I was twenty-six years old and had no significant business experience. I'd played competitive golf from age thirteen all the way through college, which served me well because I got the scholarships I needed to afford my education. My service in the Marine Corps was invaluable, but not the same as having a civilian job. I took extra courses so I could finish the MBA program in eighteen months, rather than two years. I did most of my studying at home with Susan and the baby. I approached business school as if it were a job. My task was to do well in school so I could get the best possible opportunity when I graduated. It was not like being in college. There were no parties, no football games, and no wasted hours.

My favorite course at the GSB[3] was the Theory of Finance taught by Eugene Fama and Merton Miller, who became legendary Nobel Prize winners and pioneers in theoretical finance. The lectures were inspiring, and both professors were great speakers. The courses, 431 and 432, were highly quantitative, but by the time I took them, my capability in calculus, which I had struggled with early on, had risen to respectable, and I aced them both.

My first accounting course was memorable for a couple of reasons. The professor, a gifted lecturer, called me aside and told me my questions in class were outstanding, better than anyone else's. However, on the midterm, my first exam at the GSB, I was so nervous I misunderstood the main question and got zero points on it. Embarrassingly, it was the professor's restatement of a question I'd asked in class! My first term was reminiscent of OCS; the "50 percent" pressure loomed. Halfway through my second quarter, I turned a corner and, from that point on, made the Dean's list every term.

I also took calculus during my first quarter. A PhD candidate in economics named Hodson Thornber taught the class. He

---

3   The University of Chicago Graduate School of Business.

was a striking individual, over six feet tall with shoulder-length blond hair, but he was a confusing lecturer. I came to understand that brilliant people are not necessarily good at expressing themselves. Hod made it more difficult for me to come to terms with calculus. I had taken the easy way in high school, never learning the basics of algebra and geometry. I paid the price with calculus. I had to approach Hod after every class and "beg" him for help. In that process, we became friends. We were approximately the same age, and he loved to berate me about Vietnam. He couldn't believe I had been a Marine and supported US foreign policy. It took me a while to acknowledge he was right about the war.

I managed to get a C in the course, one of two I received at the GSB. Hod and I stayed in touch, and he did occasional consulting for me when I worked at Lehman Brothers, as did Gene Fama. My other C was in macroeconomics, taught by Reuben Kessel, a respected economist. He must have been so bright that he, like Hod Thornber, had difficulty communicating his thoughts. After a three-essay final exam, I remember the entire class complaining it was impossible to understand what his questions had to do with anything we had studied or discussed in class.

We had a month off at the end of my first quarter in early September 1966, and my father found me a job as a laborer on a construction site. Foolishly, I stepped off a pick-up truck into an empty wheelbarrow, which flipped me up in the air, and I landed on my back. I had to quit the job, but fortunately, the injury was muscular, and within a few days I was feeling fine. I was too embarrassed to ask if I could go back to work, so I called an old friend who was the assistant golf professional at the Glen View Club. He said nothing was going on out there, so I should come and play. We played the back nine first, and as we came up to the first tee, there was a man and his young son preparing to tee off. He invited us to join them, and we played the front nine together.

The man was very friendly and asked me to tell him about myself. I told him about Penn and Western Illinois, Northwestern and the Marines, and at the end of the round, he gave me his business card and said, "If you ever would be interested in a job, call me." His name was Donald Perkins. He was the Chairman of the Board of the Jewel Food Stores Company in Chicago. I was unsophisticated, to say the least, and my first reaction was that I hadn't come all this way to go to work for a supermarket company. However, I researched Jewel and learned it was one of the most respected companies in Chicago and a highly desirable place to work. So when winter came, I called Mr. Perkins to see if there might be a job available that summer. I told him I was interested in a career in finance. Mr. Perkins remembered our time together at Glen View, and a few days later, offered me a job working with Jewel's treasurer in the LaSalle Street office in the financial district of downtown Chicago. He said they had never hired anyone to work in finance before, only marketing.

I told him I was extremely appreciative and excited to have a chance to work with the company during the summer. I was able to take two courses at night in the business school's evening program and work during the day for Jewel.

Working for Jewel proved an outstanding experience, as the LaSalle Street office was the headquarters for the top officers of the company, as well as the treasury staff. Every day, one of the top officers took me to lunch. I got to know them all, and it was a special experience for someone who had come from nowhere with no background in business. The two courses I took at night, linear programming and management psychology, did not interest me, and I remember nothing about either except there was an enormous amount of work and weekends were pretty much devoted to studying.

At the end of the summer, Jewel offered me a full-time job in their management training program. I was the first to receive an offer in that program, which would lead to working in finance. Obviously, my summer had been a good one, and I was extremely honored to have received such feedback from a first-class group of people running a top company. However, by that time, I had learned about investment banking. There were no courses on investment banking at business school, but a friend, Bob McCormack, who had been in the Navy and started business school the same time as I did, was from a prominent family with ties to the Northern Trust Company and an investment bank named Dillon Read. I knew I wanted to work in finance from the courses I took at school, and Bob provided enlightening information about investment banking. I thought investment banking would be a good fit because I was comfortable dealing with people, I could sell, and I was analytical. Therefore, I figured I could function in the uncertain environment of the capital markets.

I told the people at Jewel how much I appreciated their offer, but I had decided to go to New York and try investment banking because if I didn't, I would always wonder if I should have. They said they would have loved to have me but understood how I felt.

They also said Jewel had two investment bankers on their board of directors. I had spent the summer at Jewel designing a computer program to measure the investment performance of their pension fund, which was managed by the Continental Bank of Chicago. I had never heard of a board of directors. They said they liked both investment bankers but preferred one to the other. They said the one from Lehman Brothers, Stephen DuBrul, helps them figure out what to do with their business while the other, Stan Miller from Goldman Sachs, is more interested in earning fees—and asked if I would like to meet Stephen DuBrul. Of course, I said yes!

I had some interviews on campus and received a job offer from Smith Barney. I also received an offer from the Continental Bank. They offered me $13,000, which was the highest offer I received. Smith Barney asked me to go to New York to interview at its head office. I was able to coordinate my meeting with Steve DuBrul for the same trip. I was invited to lunch at Lehman Brothers with Steve and his partner, Bob Rubin, who was in charge of the Industrial Department (once again a misnomer). I arrived and was ushered into a small dining room with a table set for three. I sat at the head of the table, flanked by the two Lehman partners. The main thing I remember about the lunch is the waiter, who wore a tuxedo and held a silver tureen and a ladle. He poured onion soup into a cup in front of me, then produced a small silver bowl that held a white powdery substance, which he offered to me. I had never experienced anything like this and was confused about what to do. Should I take a spoonful and put it in the saucer, or did it belong in the soup? I decided it didn't make much sense to put it in the saucer, so I put it in the soup. Luckily, the cheese goes into the onion soup, neither of which had I ever seen before. Lunch with the two partners must have gone relatively well, and I'm sure Jewel gave me a strong recommendation because Bob Rubin offered me a job a few days later. It was for $10,000 a year, which was the lowest of all the offers I received. I never hesitated as I realized where I was going to work was more important than a few thousand dollars in starting salary. I took the job and started at Lehman on January 3, 1968.

The University of Chicago ethos has been an important

aspect of my life. I discovered finance at the Graduate School of Business and enjoyed a long and satisfying career as a result. I worked hard, and my MBA augmented the general level of self-confidence that service in the Marine Corps provided. When I showed up at Lehman, I was excited and confident. The "50 percent" factor was dead and buried.

THE JOY OF GOLF

OVER THE COURSE OF MY LIFETIME, I'VE BEEN A member of a dozen golf clubs, won twenty-seven club championships, had eight holes-in-one, and at one point held the course record for the mini golf course on Hayman Island, Australia, opposite the Great Barrier Reef. The values of the game—integrity, honor, commitment, precision, pursuit of excellence, and the will to win—relate closely to the values I hold dear to my life and career. Succeeding in junior golf from age thirteen to seventeen gave me a critical sliver of positive self-image during those challenging years. My skill got me to Western Illinois and Northwestern, where I had life-changing experiences. I met Don Perkins randomly on the golf course, and we connected. My summer experience at Jewel led to a job at Lehman Brothers, which never would have happened without meeting Don. One of my closest friends, Chas Phillips, suggested I join the National Golf Links which led to my fantastic years at Morgan Stanley, thus enabling me to start Gleacher & Company and enjoy the business experience of a lifetime.

NORTHWESTERN

The press covered my 1995 donation of $15 million to The University of Chicago, which was the second-largest ever made to the school. A sizable article ran in the *Chicago Tribune*, which did not go unnoticed at Northwestern. I immediately received a call from Henry Bienen, the President of Northwestern, who said, "Why don't we know you?" I told Henry his question was a good one because I had been giving money to Northwestern's golf program for years, yet I had never heard from the development office or from him! I told him The University of Chicago had followed my career almost from graduation, and as a result, I had relationships with many of the deans of the business school as well as the presidents of the university.

Henry Bienen was seated in my office in New York a day and a half later. I told him my opportunity to attend Northwestern changed my life, and I wanted to do something impactful for the school. Henry's personality was infectious; I liked him right away. He was obviously a renaissance man—economist, university president, elite squash competitor, and super passionate sports fan. Cool guy. Years later, he joined the board of directors of Gleacher & Company. I told Henry I would focus on what I would like to do at Northwestern and get back to him.

I called Pat Goss, Northwestern's twenty-seven-year-old golf coach. Pat was so young and freckle-faced I'm sure he had never shaved. He was an alum who had played for Northwestern and had served as assistant coach under Jeff Mory, who resigned to become head pro at Conway Farms, a new private club in Lake Forest. They continued to work as a team, and when Pat returned my call, both were on the phone. They knew exactly what they needed: an indoor practice and training facility. I was not surprised, having experienced winter in Evanston myself. An indoor facility on campus would enhance recruiting and make winter a productive time for players and coaches. I said I would call Henry and ask for some land on campus on which to build a great golf center.

Henry just laughed. He said there was not a square inch of uncommitted land on campus, but he had another option that might work. The old swimming pool and adjacent area in Patten Gym on the north side of campus lay dormant. We could have this space if it was large enough to fit our needs. Fortunately, it was. We built the first Gleacher Golf Center there twenty-three years ago (as of writing this book in 2020). It was the first indoor golf training facility in the NCAA.

We dedicated the facility in 1998, and I made a speech. I pointed out that this was not a recreational facility and was for the use of the men's and women's teams exclusively. I said building the facility was about winning. It was understood anyone Northwestern put on the field would know how to comply with proper etiquette and sportsmanship. We wanted to prove that we had the will to win and be among the very best college golf programs in the country.

Since the Gleacher Center opened, the teams have achieved seventy-five All-Big Ten selections, seven Big Ten individual champions, seven Big Ten team champions, and fourteen All-Americans. Luke Donald won the NCAA individual championship and, as a professional, was ranked number one in the world for fifty-six weeks. Luke was the first player to become the leading money winner on the PGA and European Tours in the same year and has won over $40 million playing professional golf. Luke has been a member of five undefeated European Ryder Cup teams and has fifteen professional victories worldwide.

Gleacher Center alums have won a World Golf Championship, won on the PGA Tour, European Tour, Korn Ferry Tour, Asian Tour, Canadian Tour, and PGA Tour China. Matt Fitzpatrick won five times on the European Tour by age twenty-four and was a member of his first Ryder Cup team at age twenty-one. Matt was ranked seventeenth in the world in September 2020. David Lipsky has won twice on the European Tour, twice on the Asian Tour, and once on the Korn Ferry Tour.

Last November, we opened an enlarged and redesigned Gleacher Golf Center. It cost $7 million. The video "Northwestern – Gleacher Golf Center Dedication" can be found on YouTube.[4]

Pat Goss, Emily Fletcher, and David Inglis are outstanding coaches and have been honored with many awards by the Big Ten and the coaching world. All three have become great friends, and we know we have each other's backs and would step up immediately if there was a reason to help one another.

LUKE DONALD

When the first Gleacher Golf Center opened, Luke Donald was a sophomore. Pat is still his coach, and like the rest of us, Luke continues to work on improving his game. He often visits the golf center to compare old videos of his swing to how he currently swings.

Luke and I have been partners in three AT&T Pro-Ams at Pebble Beach and a couple of Dunhill Links Pro-Ams at St. Andrews. I watched Luke shoot what looked like an effortless 10 under par 62 at Spyglass Hill during the AT&T, which is still the course record. Luke was 17 under par and held the 54-hole lead in the 2004 Dunhill. We were in the final group on Sunday, paired with David Howell, a top English pro, and Samuel L. Jackson, who needs no introduction. *Pulp Fiction* is my favorite movie, so on the third or fourth hole, walking

---

4   Here is a link to a video: https://youtu.be/ejlPbg_fGpY.

along with Samuel L., I started to recite a bit of the dialogue between Sam and John Travolta having breakfast in the diner: "You want some bacon?" "No, I don't dig on swine." "Why, you Jewish?" "No, pigs is filthy animals..." Sam laughed and said every day, at least one person asks him to record his Ezekial speech for the voicemail message on their phone!

We had a most enjoyable loop around St. Andrews that Sunday. David Howell topped Luke by one stroke but lost in a playoff to Stephen Gallacher, a Scottish pro. On the plane back to New York that night, Luke and I and our wives were having dinner, and the wine was flowing. I asked Luke how he could be so relaxed after coming up a stroke short. He explained that he had hit the ball fine in the final round, but his putts didn't fall as they had the first three days. He was confident he would have many more chances to win. I marveled at his composure.

NICK FALDO

Nick and his girlfriend, Brenna, were staying with us during the 1997 PGA Championship at Winged Foot. We were talking after dinner, and I asked Nick where he got his hair cut in London, where I spent a lot of time. He told me, and I asked how a celebrity like himself tipped. He said, "I don't tip." Immediately, Brenna said, "Well, hell, Nick, that's why it takes so long to get the car at the hotel!" Nick was a killer competitor on the golf course but a very funny guy, with a dry sense of humor when he was relaxed. He is probably the most efficient and precise striker of the ball I have ever played with.

VIJAY SINGH

Luke and I were paired with Vijay and Teddy Forstmann in the AT&T. We were playing at Spyglass Hill. Vijay made a very ugly triple-bogey 8 on the par 5 seventh hole. I had a 9-iron for my third shot and almost holed it, leaving it about a foot from the pin. It was the first time I had played with Vijay, and I knew his reputation for being difficult. I was walking behind him up the slight hill toward the eighth tee, and he turned around and said, "That was a great shot you hit back there and a super birdie." So much for reputations. After a triple-bogey on a hole where he figures to make a birdie, Vijay makes an amateur feel like a million bucks, unsolicited. I was really impressed. I don't think I would be capable of doing that right after making a triple-bogey.

BEN CRENSHAW

In the mid-1970s, I joined seven other men for golf at Pine Valley. We stayed in a house on the property owned by a Texas oilman who had put together the group. Darrell Royal, the legendary University of Texas football coach was with us, as were Ben Crenshaw and David Graham, major champions who were visiting Pine Valley for the first time. We played thirty-six holes a day for four consecutive days, rearranging the pairings for each round. Ben was scheduled to play in a PGA Tour event at Westchester CC the following week, and I was going back to the office in New York, so I drove Ben up to White Plains where he was staying. As we drove up the New Jersey Turnpike, I said, "Ben, everyone would agree that you are among the best putters in golf, maybe *the* best. I'm frustrated because my ball-striking is pretty good, but my putting is not at the same level. We have just played a number of rounds together, so you have seen me hit a lot of putts. Please give me something to try, and I will do whatever you recommend." At least thirty seconds of silence ensued, it seemed much longer, and finally Ben responded, "Eric, a putt is just a little shot. That's all there is to it. Just roll the ball."

Ben, like all of the best putters I have known, and like Luke Donald, who is certainly in Ben's league, is not mechanical. The best putters just putt. They may have drills they do in practice, but in competitions, they just roll the ball. I'm still searching for the key to that kingdom!

RAFAEL NADAL

Early one morning, I received a phone call from Dirk Ziff, a friend of many years. Dirk told me Tony Godsick had called and asked if he would take Rafael Nadal to play golf. Tony is Roger Federer's agent, and Rafa and Roger are close friends. Nadal had arrived the night before from Beijing after winning the gold medal in singles in the 2008 Olympics. He was in town for the upcoming US Open but wanted some R&R beforehand. Dirk was flying to Brazil that morning and asked if I would like to play golf with Nadal. I had things to do but nothing that couldn't be rescheduled.

I picked up Rafa at his hotel on Central Park South. Nike had opened their 57th St. store early so Rafa could pick up some golf clothes and shoes. As we were driving out to Deepdale in the morning traffic, I could not help but think if I had an accident and he was injured, it would be an international disaster for us both!

We arrived at the first tee, and I offered to keep score. Rafa said that he always kept his own score. I remembered his habit of lining up the bottles of water in some precise way when competing, so I understood. He played right-handed even though he plays tennis left-handed. He is ambidextrous, as are many world-class athletes. He does most things right-handed but the spin coming off a left-handed serve is advantageous in championship tennis. Rafa shot 82 and holed every putt. I played well and scored 75. We had lunch and talked about all kinds of things—sports, world affairs, women, etc. Rafa is an outstanding individual, well-rounded, and not at all full of himself. I was thoroughly impressed. We both enjoyed a wonderful day.

Tony Godsick called me the next morning. He thanked me

and passed on appreciation from Rafa. Then he said, "You'll like this." Rafa had told him, referring to my golf game, "That Mr. Eric, he's so good."

ARNOLD PALMER

In 1999, I received the Rolex Achievement Award. This award is presented annually to a former college golfer who has achieved excellence in his or her career outside of golf and, in doing so, has made a special contribution to society. Dan Quayle and Mark McCormick were the recipients in the two years preceding my award.

My wife, Annie, and I flew to Wake Forest, NC, and had dinner with Arnold and Winnie Palmer the evening before the presentation. The King had attended Wake Forest prior to serving in the Coast Guard and turning pro, and he was a loyal supporter of the school and its golf program. Dinner was relaxed and enjoyable. Winnie was a lovely person, and Arnold had that wonderful gift that money cannot buy: the ability to relate to people and make them feel like they occupy 100 percent of his attention and interest.

During dinner, I told Arnold that I might have seen him play his first competitive round as a professional. He participated in an exhibition match at Sewells Point in Norfolk shortly after winning the 1954 US Amateur at CC of Detroit and turning pro. He and John O'Donnell, my first coach, played

Chandler Harper and Ira Templeton, an amateur from Tennessee, and prevailed in a close match. Arnold said no one had ever brought that match up with him, but he remembered the occasion even though he had not thought about it in many years. It was his first appearance as a professional golfer, and he shot sixty-seven. I told him I was fourteen at the time, and I had not seen anyone hit a golf ball the way he did. His athleticism and power seemed unbelievable to me, as did the size and obvious strength of his hands and forearms. I told Arnold I could still see a clear image of him striking his tee shot on the first hole of the match and hear the sound of his driver compressing the ball. He loved the story.

The following day at the presentation, Arnold handed me a beautiful Rolex watch and made some brief remarks about my golf and business careers. All in all, it was an experience I had thanks to my philanthropy—financing the first golf training facility in the NCAA at Northwestern—and one that would not have happened without the impact golf had on my life.

THE USGA

I was recruited to become a member of the USGA Executive Committee by Ernie Ransome, the long-time President of Pine Valley Golf Club near Philadelphia, where I also was a member. The television contract associated with the US

Open had grown exponentially, and the USGA had no one capable of investing the significant cash inflow. Starting with $10 million of investable funds, over four years, I built a $400 million portfolio. The USGA should never again have to worry about money.

I attended rules school for referees and scored ninety-eight on the three-and-a-half-hour rules exam. I officiated in seventeen major championships—eight US Opens, seven Masters, one British Open, and one PGA Championship. Watching the best in the world up close was a rare opportunity that validated my decision years earlier to go to school rather than play professional golf!

I was a member of the championship committee that selected the US Open venues. At my first meeting, the committee was about to dismiss Bethpage Black as a potential site. David Fay, the Executive Director, and his staff had advocated aggressively for Bethpage, but no member of the decision-making committee had seen the course. I explained to the group that I had played in the Metropolitan Golf Association stroke play championship at Bethpage Black and felt the course was stupendous. I suggested before removing it from the "potential" list, a group from the committee should play the course. Fred Ridley, who is now Chairman of Augusta National, and three others played nine holes in a hard, cold spring rain, which caused them to forgo the second nine. Even so, the group was thoroughly impressed with the course, and Bethpage was promptly confirmed as the site of the 2002 Open. The USGA spent more than $3 million renovating the course without asking New York State to repay anything. Bethpage is open to the public and is part of the New York State Parks system. I believe the 2002 US Open, which Tiger Woods won and which averaged 55,000 people in attendance per day, was one of the greatest ever. The press called it "The People's Open."

The USGA museum was located in Liberty Corner, NJ. More deer looked through the windows than paying customers walked through the doors. I was given responsibility for the museum and tried to move it to New York City, where 55 million tourists visited each year. The USGA bought the Russian Tea Room on 57th Street right next to Carnegie Hall. It had an ideal footprint and a location second to none. Unfortunately, the city presented many onerous requirements, and the USGA bureaucracy couldn't even agree on who was going to design the museum. Eventually, they abandoned the initiative and sold the Russian Tea Room for a $3 million profit. The USGA built a new $22 million museum at Liberty Corner after I was gone. The deer continued to record much higher attendance than the public.

The worst USGA blunder I was party to involved Bandon Dunes and its three golf courses. Mike Keiser, the owner and developer of Bandon Dunes on the southern Oregon coast, asked me to spend a couple of days with him on the site. It was amazing—spectacular views and great golfing all in one magical location. Mike said he wanted to "give" Bandon Dunes to the USGA. He did not want a developer to get control of the property after he was gone and build houses around the golf courses. I created a structure that would have returned Mike's cash investment plus a substantial tax deduction, which he could use in the future when he sold the greeting card company he owned.

Mike wanted to complete the deal, but the executive committee, directed by the omnipresent group of "past presidents," turned it down because Bandon Dunes was "competitive" with USGA member clubs. The octogenarian past presidents, who dominated the committee meetings and intimidated all but the most self-confident members (each member had to be nominated to the committee annually, and the eighty-plus-year-olds did the nominating), had simply created an implausible excuse to reject the opportunity. The approximately 8,000 USGA member clubs they were "concerned" about each paid the grand sum of $40 a year in dues to be members of the USGA! (Dues today are $150 per year per club.) The elderly contingent was unable to process the obvious benefit of accepting a self-sufficient West Coast location (the USGA is very East Coast centric) with three championship courses suitable for hosting one or a few USGA championships every year.

I had dinner with Mike Keiser and his wife at a wedding

in Chicago not long ago, and we laughed about the USGA rejection. In retrospect, it was a stroke of good luck for Mike. He continued developing Bandon Dunes, which now has six courses and is one of the premier golf destinations in the world.

The USGA held the US Men's Amateur Championship at Bandon in 2020.

TIGER WOODS

Tiger Woods was playing his first-round match in the 1996 US Amateur Championship in Pumpkin Ridge, OR. He had won the previous two US Amateurs and was favored to win his third in a row. He was a skinny twenty-year-old and looked nothing like he does now. I had never seen him play and was excited to referee his first-round match. Tiger's opponent was an All American from San Jose State, an outstanding player. They halved the first three holes, and on the fourth, Tiger blew his tee shot eighty yards past his opponent; I paced it off. Tiger hit a 6-iron onto the par 5 green and never looked back. That tee shot completely deflated his opponent, and Tiger did not miss a shot during the match and won easily. It was a clinic, and I was amazed at the level of golfing excellence I had witnessed.

I was scheduled to return to New York the next morning but was so struck by what I had seen, I decided to stick around and watch the first few holes of Tiger's second-round match against Charles Howell. Charles was around the same age as Tiger, had been a standout junior player, and was playing college golf for Oklahoma State. I thought this would be a true test for Tiger.

They were off at 8 a.m., and at least 5,000 fans made a complete ring around the first hole. I was standing under a tree near the first green. Tiger's mother, Kultida, was standing nearby. She recognized me from the day before and said, "You referee this match?" I told her no, but I thought it would be a good match because Charles Howell was a top player. This seemed to offend her, and a silence evolved. Then she replied, "Tiger say show me what you got, then I show you what I got." That ended our morning chat! No question where Tiger's will to win came from.

Tiger beat Charles Howell and went on to win his third straight US Amateur and his sixth straight USGA championship when combined with the three consecutive US junior championships he won between the ages of fifteen and seventeen. I do not believe anyone else will ever accomplish this feat.

The following spring at the historic 1997 Masters, I interacted once again with Tiger. I was the rules official at the par 5 15th green on Sunday, and Tiger's second shot came to rest up against a canvas bag in the gallery to the right of the green. Tiger carefully moved the bag away from his ball. Both of us were bent over, looking intently to determine if the ball had moved from its position. I said, "I don't think it moved." Tiger agreed, pitched his ball onto the green, and made his par. He won by the astounding margin of twelve strokes, the first of five Masters he has won thus far. I was amazed at how relaxed he was when we went through the procedure with the canvas bag, as the feeling in the air was electric with excitement about his extraordinary achievement that was about to become history. Tiger was deep in the "zone."

When I arrived back at the rules headquarters, the tournament chairman called me into his office and told me that more than three hundred people had called in to report that with ultra-slow motion HD, it was apparent that Tiger's ball had moved slightly when he moved the bag. I said Tiger and I did not feel the ball moved. And that was all that mattered.

PAULA

Most important of all is how I met my fantastic wife, Paula. My friend Dick Gilbert's wife, Zena, introduced us because Paula and I were both good golfers. I had been separated more than a year from my wife, Annie, following a long marriage. The first time Paula and I met, we played golf at Shinnecock, a difficult US Open venue. I suggested a match, gave her three shots a nine, played as hard as I could, and we ended up all even. I had the home course advantage because she had never played Shinnecock. I was impressed with her golf and her competitiveness. It was clear she had no interest in losing.

I was also impressed with other aspects of her presence. She is beautiful, and that day was wearing a pair of the shortest golf shorts I had ever seen. My friend and regular caddy at Shinnecock, Eric Ryder, was aware of my impending divorce and various aspects of my social life. As Paula addressed her second shot to the 13th green, I asked Eric, "What do you think?" Without a nanosecond of hesitation, he replied, "Are you kidding?!" That says it all.

It took a while, but the die was cast. Paula likes to be in control, and when we first started dating, she refused to allow me to pick her up at her home. After a few weeks, her son, Cameron, asked if she was losing her mind, so she finally relented. This is our fifteenth year together, and it keeps getting better. While she likes complete control, I like to delegate—so it works out. We continue to play each other for $10, but now we play even, no strokes. Paula has won eighteen club championships, but most of our friends would say her painting is far more impressive than her golf. Thank you, Golf Gods, for delivering her into my life!

Dad circa 1910

Grandpa

Dad-Joe Morgan 1921

Dad–Student Boxer 1921

Grandpa's house circa 1950

Grandpa fishing circa 1950

USMC shooting badges 1965

grass of the bunker, and Gleacher lifted it nicely onto the green up to within 10 feet of the pin. He wasn't afraid of the greens, as he charged the putt and ran it over the lip of the cup, leaving right up to six inches from the green, however, and his sixth par.

Challenger Robbins

One of the best bets to take away Gleacher's title is PI's Dick Robbins.

GLEACHER ON FOURTH FAIRWAY
Defending Champion Blasts Three Iron To Green

Defending Champion 1966

Dad circa 1985

First win 1953

JUNE 1953

THEY WON PRIZES TOO—Here are eight of the prize winners in the State Junior Amateur Golf Tournament completed yesterday at Hidden Valley Country Club. They are (l. to r.)

(World-News Staff Photo)

front — Danny Keffer, Gayle Naff, Rickey Gleacher and Charles Holden; second—Stuart Wallace, Walter Lawrence, III, Calvin Sisson and Alvin Rose.

Second win 1953

National Champions Western Illinois 1959

Interservice tournament 1965

With Peter Burt (far left) and Gene Goodwillie (3rd from left) at Muirfield 1979

With Jimmy at British Senior Amateur 1998

With Arnold Palmer having won the Rolex Achievement Award 1998

With Luke Donald, World #1

With all six children 1992

72ND GREEN, MUIRFIELD, SCOTLAND
10:20 PM JUNE 10, 2004
BRITISH OPEN IN A DAY

All four sons play 72 holes in one day at Muirfield 2004

Sarah, John, and Jimmy 1995

Sarah graduates from medical school 1987

Summer dinner with Paula, Jay, Patsy, and Willy 2014

Cameron (Paula's son) graduates from college

Paula—the golfing girl 2009

Congratulations! Eric... This is truly a major win! Hope to see you soon~ [signature]

Nat West to Buy Gleacher
In $135 Million Stock Deal

By PETER TRUELL

National Westminster Bank P.L.C., the British bank that is remolding its American business, said yesterday that it would issue $135 million in new shares to acquire Gleacher & Company, a New York investment bank that specializes in mergers and acquisitions.

The acquired company, which will be known as Gleacher NatWest, will become "the principal focus of NatWest's investment banking operation in North America," NatWest said in a statement. Eric J. Gleacher, the firm's founder, will become chairman of NatWest Markets North America, the NatWest group's American investment bank, which now employs 1,100 people.

"The objective here is to build a substantial domestic investment banking business," said Peter J. Hall, president and chief executive officer of NatWest Markets North America. "And that really is a fundamental part of our global strategy, which is to build a top 10 global investment bank. We're really looking to Eric to be the ambassador, the man with the client relationship."

Mr. Gleacher said: "We think the amalgamation of their capital markets capability and our mergers and acquisition skills will be very strong. Going forward it's going to be more of a one-stop shopping approach to this business."

In the last 12 months, Gleacher has advised on several large mergers and acquisitions, including the $10 billion purchase of American Cyanamid by American Home Products and the $670 million acquisition of Kidder, Peabody by Paine Webber. Gleacher has also consulted British Airways about its stake in USAir Group.

National Westminster, Britain's second-largest commercial bank after Barclays, is negotiating to sell NatWest Bancorp, its retail commercial banking business in New York and New Jersey, for as much as $4 billion, cutting back its American retail banking as it builds its capital markets and investment banking.

Some bank analysts seemed relieved at NatWest's deal for Gleacher, in part because they said it implied that NatWest would not be spending billions of dollars to buy a big New York investment bank.

"This is a sensible way of trying to exit the commercial bank and get into investment banking," said Christopher C. Ellerton, bank analyst at the London office of SBC Warburg, a unit of the Swiss Bank Corporation. "Shareholders will be relieved if this is all they plan to spend to get into investment banking," he added, noting that there had been speculation recently that NatWest might buy Salomon Brothers or Lehman Brothers, both of which would now be valued in the billions of dollars.

The acquisition of Gleacher with newly issued shares should not dilute current National Westminster shares, provided that the acquired unit earns at least $14 million a year, Mr. Ellerton said.

Gleacher & Company, which has 38 employees, previously had an informal agreement with Deutsche Morgan Grenfell, the investment banking unit of Deutsche Bank A.G., to refer merger and acquisition business to each other. That agreement, established five years ago, ended this week, a spokeswoman for Deutsche Morgan Grenfell said, adding that the German bank would continue to build its own mergers and acquisitions capability in North America.

Gleacher sells to NatWest 1995

Another Win 2018

LEHMAN BROTHERS 1968–1983

———

I GRADUATED FROM THE UNIVERSITY OF CHICAGO IN December 1967. I had a wife, a one-year-old son, and no money. I called Bob Rubin at Lehman and asked if the firm provided assistance with moving expenses for new employees. In his low-key way, Bob said he'd never heard of anything like that but would ask around if I wanted him to. I immediately said no, it would not be necessary. Much to my surprise, I learned the student loan program provided moving assistance with low-interest charges. I borrowed $3,000 and started planning the move to New York.

Lehman Brothers was an eclectic place in the late 1960s, located in a triangular building in lower Manhattan at One William Street across from Delmonico's restaurant. The entire firm comprised about 400 people. It was a short walk up from the Staten Island ferry, which was how I commuted to work. There were only sixteen people in the Industrial

Department, and there were exactly sixteen desks. For the first few months, I would come in every day and find a vacant desk whose regular user was out of town. This enabled me to get to know most of the people in the department. There was one other young associate whom the Chicago office had sent to New York for training. Unfortunately, he was not cut out to be a Lehman associate, and he departed. I was assigned his desk. One of the unusual aspects of the Lehman culture was that every six or nine months the office chairs were shuffled. All the offices had two desks facing each other, and none were large. People were able to observe how others worked and how they talked to clients on the phone. This was beneficial for me since my learning curve was vertical. A short time after I got my first desk, we shuffled. I was partnered with Bill Morris, an MIT graduate a few years older than me. He was a very nice guy, and we got along well. I remember one piece of advice Bill passed on to me. He said, "Don't make any mistakes, and you'll get to be a partner." My reaction at the time (to myself) was that I didn't come to play it safe; I came to see what I could accomplish. Fortunately, I didn't make any serious mistakes, and I became a partner in five years. Bill's advice was prudent, but my personality did not match with risk-averse existence.

Lehman in those days was a tribal environment: Herman and Sidney Kahn, father and son; Joe and Michael Thomas, father and son. Whatever Herman did for Sidney, Joe did for Michael. Both sons became partners in three years. Many associates doing excellent work in the Industrial Department were dismayed by the nepotism, and some left Lehman for new jobs. Special financial deals that partners had negotiated with Robert Lehman, head of the firm, caused jealousy and strife. The terms usually became known, and those who didn't have a similar arrangement felt slighted. The firm was an amalgamation of exceptional talent. People who started their careers at Lehman made up a Who's Who of Wall Street. Lehman had the deepest talent pool on the street embedded in a defective, non-teamwork, eat-what-you-kill, every-man-for-himself culture. Eventually, Lehman's business trajectory became illustrative of a Warren Buffett axiom: good manager, bad business—bad business always wins.

After I had been with Lehman for a year or so, I was "discovered" by Lewis Glucksman, who built and ran Lehman's commercial paper business. Financing companies' short-term cash requirements with commercial paper was a big business, and for many substantial companies, the only way they connected with Wall Street. Lew was a rough and tough trader. He was from the Lower East Side of Manhattan and did not interface well with the partners from the Upper East Side. Lew was in by 6 a.m. every morning and read all the newspapers before trading commenced. He would invariably have egg on his tie or shirt, his collar was never buttoned, and once, when I was sitting with him, something caused him to rise and scream at Gloria Markfeld, the treasurer of the commercial paper business. This emotional reflex action combined with Lew's sizable belly caused most of the buttons of his shirt to pop off like bullets from a rifle! You couldn't make this up!

Lew was a great supporter of mine. I was different. I did not go to Yale, Harvard, or Princeton like most of the men in investment banking (there were no women) and had been a Marine infantry officer. I had life experiences with real people, unlike most of the Ivy League contingent in the firm. I was young and inexperienced but a quick learner. Lew began to include me when he met with commercial paper issuers who might become investment banking clients. The result was an inflow of significant business, which was very positive for us both. I was in my late twenties and loved it. I had no fear of making mistakes or failing.

Nestlé was a commercial paper client and was having problems with Libby, McNeil and Libby, a partially-owned subsidiary.[5] Nestlé was headquartered in Vevey, Switzerland, and had few relationships with American investment banks. Libby was a US company and hired Morgan Stanley to represent them. Bob Greenhill was the Morgan partner working for Libby. Bob and I met in New York one afternoon and concluded we could not advance negotiations unless we met with Nestlé and clarified certain issues. We booked a TWA flight that evening to Geneva. We met with Eric Gabus

---

5   A company owning less than 100 percent but more than 50 percent of the common stock in another company.

of Nestlé the next day in Vevey and sorted everything out. This was my first trip to Europe, and at age twenty-nine, I was representing one of the most important companies in the world in a complicated and visible transaction. Nestlé acquired control of Libby through a rights offering[6] followed by a tender offer[7] for all remaining publicly held shares of common stock. This solved all problems. Other significant business with Nestlé followed, including the acquisition of Stouffer Foods, which is still part of Nestlé today.

In 1970, we helped McDonnell Douglas (MD) finance the DC-10 aircraft program. Similar to Nestlé, MD was a commercial paper client with no significant investment banking relationships. George W. Ball, a senior Lehman partner who had been Under Secretary of State for Presidents John F. Kennedy and Lyndon Johnson, had a relationship with "Mr. Mac," as James McDonnell was known. George and I flew to St. Louis to meet him at MD's headquarters at the airport. I was introduced as the Lehman banker who would work with MD to create a financing plan for the DC-10 program. At the time, there were three major aircraft manufacturers ramping up production of a new generation of aircraft. Boeing had the 747, Lockheed the L-1011, and MD the DC-10. All were new generations of wide-bodied, long-range planes

---

6   A company offering its shareholders an opportunity to buy newly issued common stock usually at a discount to current market value.

7   A bid almost always in cash for shares of another company which, if unopposed, can be completed in approximately thirty days.

that would revolutionize air travel for leisure and business and would have a major positive effect on the world economy. The challenge was to raise the money to build and test a prototype aircraft so an order book could be established with airlines all over the world. The cost of doing so was approximately a billion dollars per company, a staggering amount for the banking system to service fifty years ago.

I had many meetings with Mr. Mac to go over plans that my team had created. I was always met at the bottom of the TWA ramp by his driver, who would take me across the airport to the headquarters building. If we were having lunch, we would walk from Mr. Mac's office across an enormous open floor full of engineers drafting plans for various components of the 10. Mr. Mac knew everyone—and I mean *everyone*—and greeted them by their first names. He was seventy years old, and we enjoyed a very good relationship. One evening at dinner in St. Louis, he asked how old I was. It flashed through my mind that if I told the truth, the answer might affect our relationship. I told the truth and said I was thirty. He did not comment, but I was sure my age caused a bit of a shock. There was no repercussion, but I sensed thereafter a subtle coolness when we were together.

We successfully financed the DC-10 program. However, the oversupply caused by too many competitors eventually sank MD and Lockheed. Boeing acquired MD, and Lockheed shut down the L-1011 program and pursued other defense businesses. Working with an aerospace legend forty years my senior to solve a challenging problem was an invaluable experience.

The Ralston Purina Company, also headquartered in St. Louis, was another of Lew Gluckman's relationships. Ralston had evolved into a consumer-products company from its roots in commodity businesses such as animal feed distribution, grain milling, and broiler poultry production. Wall Street had been pressuring the company to divest these cyclical businesses, so reported earnings from branded products would become more predictable, thus enabling the stock to trade at a higher price-to-earnings ratio[8]. Ralston was aware of the work I had done with McDonnell Douglas, which, combined with Lew's relationship, got us hired. The company had a very large poultry business located in Georgia and Arkansas. I sold it in pieces to local buyers rather than to one large buyer; the aggregate price was higher that way. Hal Dean, the Ralston Chairman, was delighted.

In 1973, I helped Roger Freeman, an Englishman seconded to Lehman by one of the major accounting firms, open the first Lehman office in London. Roger was a bright, upper-middle-class Brit. He was a competent accountant and motivated to succeed. However, he was quite reserved, as are many of his countrymen, and found it difficult to connect

---

8   The market price of a common stock divided by the earnings per share of the company provides an indication of how highly regarded the stock is.

with his American colleagues at Lehman. My exposure to Europe during the Nestlé transaction had whetted my appetite for opportunities overseas. Roger and I were friends, and confidence developed between us. I committed to calling on companies with him to talk about acquisition opportunities in the US. Roger knew which UK companies fit my experience and expertise and had the proper accent to call the CEOs and get us in front of them.

One of the companies Roger called was Imperial Foods, a subsidiary of Imperial Group, one of the most substantial companies in the UK. Imperial Group also owned a tobacco company and the largest chain of pubs in Britain. Imperial Foods was a diversified food company similar to Ralston and Pillsbury, but unlike them, it wanted to expand its already substantial chicken and turkey businesses. We met with Michael Davies, the CEO, who was cerebral and knowledgeable, and we had an excellent session. Roger and I developed other significant investment banking business in the UK, but that initial meeting with Michael Davies would prove to be a game-changer.

Later that year, I received a call from Bill Spoor, whom I did not know. Bill had recently become Chairman of Pillsbury, a major food products company headquartered in Minneapolis. He had met with Hal Dean, seeking advice. Hal told him I had figured out how to get the best price for Ralston's poultry business and suggested he hire me to sell Pillsbury's. I went to Minneapolis to meet Spoor and was hired.

Mike Harper was in charge of Pillsbury's poultry business, and we worked on the financials and an executive summary of the business for Michael Davies. Mike Harper could not believe my assertion that we would sell a poultry business in Rogers, Arkansas to a major company in England. I assured him it was the likely outcome. Mike and I went to London and met with Michael Davies. We sold the business to Imperial Foods for $20 million (about $100 million in today's market.)

Mike told me he did not get along with Bill Spoor and was going to leave the company once the poultry sale was complete. He was impressed with Michael Davies and asked if he could speak to him about staying on and running the business for Imperial. I said certainly, and that conversation resulted in one of the most fortuitous breaks Mike Harper would ever get. Michael Davies said he was going to hire the founder and his son to run things because if he didn't, they might quit, and the business would suffer. Mike went on to much more significant endeavors than running the former Pillsbury poultry business. More about Mike Harper later.

THE MOONIES AND MICHAEL DAVIES

I'M INTERRUPTING THE LEHMAN NARRATIVE TO TELL the story of something that happened eight years after Michael Davies and I met.

One day in 1981, I got a call from Michael Davies, who was in London. It was not about business. Michael's son, Mark, and his friend, Victor Crutchley, had graduated from Eton and embarked on a gap-year of touring the United States. They bought a used car in New York and drove a northern route to the West Coast and six months later took a southern route back east to New York City. Mark went back to England, and Victor decided to remain in New York. Mark had a conversation with Victor before he left and thought Victor was considering joining the Moonies.[9] No one had been able to reach Victor for a few weeks. Michael said that

---

9   The Unification Church is a worldwide religious movement whose members are called Moonies.

Victor's parents were understandably quite upset and asked if there was any way I could help. Victor's parents had no contacts in the US. Michael and I had become friends over the past eight years of doing business together.

Victor was an idealistic lad drawn to theoretical projects to save the world. He had been approached in Greenwich Village by a very pretty girl and two guys, all Moonies. Michael told me Victor's father had been an admiral in the Royal Navy and was a grandson of Queen Victoria, making Victor a great-great-grandson and a person of substantial financial means. Part of one's commitment to the Moonies was turning all monies earned (we've all seen them selling flowers at traffic lights) and all other financial assets over to the cult. Victor was in the early stages of their brainwashing procedure, and it was unlikely the Moonies knew what a big fish they had on the line.

I told Michael I was all-in and took on the situation with a vengeance. I stopped whatever I was doing and trained all my focus and energy on how I could rescue this impressionable young man from a potentially disastrous situation. I had met him briefly before he and Mark Davies set off for the West Coast.

My first call was to the NYPD. I was connected to a detective who directed me to a rabbi in Brooklyn, who was devoted to extricating young people from the Moonies. This proved to be a godsend. The rabbi was smart, tough, and knew what to do. He told me the Moonies owned a building on 44th Street and suggested I go there and wait for them to show up with Victor at the end of the day and try to talk to him. He predicted they would try to keep him away from me. He emphasized it would be necessary to "persuade" Victor to leave as it was against the law to force him.

I arrived around 5 p.m. and waited across the street from the building. I had left my suit coat and tie at the office and had no briefcase. I was ready for whatever these brainwashing cult misfits wanted to bring. I felt sympathy for the Crutchley family even though I had not met them. I put myself in their shoes and realized how frightened I would be if it was my son's life at risk.

At about 8 p.m., a group of six or seven arrived, and I recognized Victor. He was tall and easy to spot. I identified myself and asked to speak with him. He looked shocked and was quickly ushered into the building. I had waited for hours and accomplished nothing. I had found Victor and confirmed he was with the Moonies, but beyond that, nothing. I was not happy. I entered the building and demanded to see someone in charge. A young man arrived, and I told him I was a friend of Victor's family and needed to talk with him. His mother was ill, and he must speak to his father. The rabbi had suggested this strategy. The Moonie said Victor couldn't see me because he was in a group meeting which would go on for some time. I told him this was a life-and-death situation, and I would be back tomorrow, and if they did not allow me to meet with Victor, all hell would come down on them. I told him Victor's father was a senior member of the British government, I was a partner at Lehman Brothers (doubtful he knew what that was), and law enforcement would deal with this situation if they prohibited Victor from speaking to his father.

I went back to my office and called the rabbi. He told me the Moonies would probably ignore my threats and claim Victor did not wish to speak to his family. He said our best chance was to bring someone over from the UK who had a relationship with Victor. Victor would have a hard time ignoring a friend who had traveled so far to see him. If they could have a private conversation, perhaps Victor could be persuaded to remove himself to see his sick mother. Victor would initially be upset that we had deceived him about his mother's condition. However, the rabbi said that deprogramming experts in the UK would immediately help him realize what a perilous situation he had avoided.

I called Michael Davies and reviewed the rabbi's advice. Within an hour, Michael reported that a don[10] from Eton who was close to Victor would be on a British Airways flight the next day. I made a hotel reservation for the don and called it a day.

---

10   A teacher at a UK university or boarding school.

I spoke to the rabbi in the morning. He explained how the don should approach his conversation with Victor. I went back to 44th Street late that afternoon. I entered the building and asked to see the person I'd interacted with the night before. He appeared in a few minutes, and I thought this might be progress. I told him a close family friend was coming from England to talk to Victor about his mother's condition. He said Victor had been moved to an upstate New York location for further training. I told him I needed to know where he was located, and to my surprise, the Moonie gave me an address. The cult must have realized if Victor's mother died, and they had not allowed him access to information about her condition, they would risk losing him in the aftermath. I had no idea if they had provided the correct location for Victor but had no choice other than to go and find out.

The upstate location was a good three hours north of New York City. My wife, Annie, and I were up early, as was the don due to the five-hour time change from the UK. He was clad in a heavy tweed suit, and the July temperature was already ninety-seven degrees. This was his first time in the US, and he seemed understandably discombobulated.

We drove north and eventually found the location, a small farm with a few buildings surrounded by woods. I approached a man who had appeared when we pulled into the driveway. I explained that a teacher from Victor's school had come from England to discuss his mother's serious medical condition. He told me Victor was out with a group but would return by lunchtime. We waited. The don moseyed around and talked to a couple of the Moonies. He seemed to relate to their cause. This didn't surprise me, but I was concerned about his effectiveness if the opportunity to speak to Victor materialized.

Victor came up the driveway with a small group of young people. When he saw the don, he looked visibly shaken. The leader of his group told him he did not have to talk to anyone if he chose not to. Our group and his stood facing each other. Victor finally came over and embraced the don and they walked out to a pasture a few hundred yards away. They stayed out there in the hot sun for almost two hours. Then they slowly walked in and approached Annie and me. The don said, "He's going to come with us." I said, "Great, let's get in the car and go!" As I was nervously pulling out of the driveway, Annie screamed that she had left her purse behind. I hit the brakes, and she jumped out of the car, collected her purse, and raced back. I made my BMW prove it deserved its reputation, and we were gone in a flash.

Cell phones did not exist, so I drove straight to Lehman Brothers to call Michael Davies. There was no sign of anyone following us, and the three-hour return trip was uneventful and quiet with no conversation. I didn't know how the Don had managed to convince Victor to leave, and I didn't ask. As soon as we reached my office, I called Michael and reported the good news. He called back minutes later and said Victor and the don were on a BA flight to London at 8 p.m. from JFK. When we arrived at the terminal, we were to identify ourselves to any BA agent and would be taken to a private room near the flight's gate area. Michael was the senior director on the British Airways board of directors, and BA had arranged for Victor to be allowed back into the UK even though his passport was with his other belongings at the Moonies' farm and he had no means of identification.

I drove to JFK, and in no time, we were in a VIP room by ourselves. Eventually, the two travelers were escorted to the plane, and Annie and I went home. What a day! I was floating in adrenaline and did not sleep much that night. We had accomplished something important which transcended business: we had done the right thing to help a friend.

I called Michael first thing in the morning. Victor had been upset when he found out his mother was in good health, but the deprogramming team had begun its work, and the rabbi was confident Victor would acknowledge he had avoided a potentially disastrous situation once presented with all the facts about the Moonies. That is exactly what happened. I thanked the rabbi profusely and sent a generous contribution to his synagogue. What a partner he had been. We would not have been able to extricate Victor without his advice.

Michael and I continued to transact significant business in

the UK. Unfortunately, he died unexpectedly in his sleep a few years later. I gave the eulogy at his service, and many of the British business elite were present, reflecting the respect Michael's peers had for him. A very sad loss of a special friend for me.

A few months after Victor came home, a package arrived from the UK. It contained a sterling silver cup engraved with the Crutchley family crest and a lovely inscription. The accompanying note included an invitation to visit the family in Dorset, where they live. Dorset is a beautiful part of England and perhaps someday I will accept their invitation. Victor eventually became a farmer and built a family with his wife. I will always remember what the rabbi, the don, and Michael and I were able to accomplish for a family facing the possible loss of a son.

LEHMAN CONTINUED

THE US ECONOMY WAS IN A CRISIS, WHICH STARTED IN 1973 and lasted through 1976–1977. OPEC had created a gasoline shortage by reducing the output of crude oil. Customers were forced to wait for hours in long lines to buy gas. It was excruciating and frustrating for busy mothers with small children, businesspeople trying to make a living, and businesses of all types trying to survive. Interest rates were 20–22 percent, a statistic impossible to fathom these days when half the world seems to function with negative rates.

Lew Glucksman had invested a substantial amount of borrowed capital in a Treasury bill position that had gone the wrong way. Interest rates had risen, thus lowering the value of the securities the firm had purchased. Thanks to this unfortunate situation, the firm was losing almost a million dollars a month in 1974.

I assumed the US economy would correct itself, as it always had in the past, and Lehman would survive the self-inflicted wound. These assumptions carried the most risk of any decision I had made in my life, as I was a highly leveraged young partner. Lehman was a paradoxical and flawed environment in many ways, dominated by multiple fiefdoms whose leaders intensely disliked each other. Leadership had experienced frequent turnover. Robert Lehman became ill and selected Joe Thomas, an outgoing and brilliant Texan and director of many important companies, to run the firm. Unfortunately, Joe also became seriously ill, and the firm, amid much turmoil, found itself under the control of Fred Ehrman, an enigmatic introvert who completely lacked leadership skills and commercial instincts. Glucksman was sitting on a bond position that could bankrupt Lehman, and he and Ehrman had no ability to interact successfully. Information about Glucksman's disastrous investment was not widely known, but it cast an ominous shadow on the future of the firm.

Glucksman had to make a move. He joined forces with James Glanville, another Texas oilman, who was Joe Thomas's protégé. Glanville was tough, supremely talented, and loathed Fred Ehrman, who he thought would run the firm into the ground. Glucksman controlled the commercial paper business, which was an important profit center, and Glanville had numerous relationships of his own, many of which he had inherited from Joe Thomas. The two of them were the most prolific moneymakers in the firm. On Wall Street, that is power.

They mounted a coup, which brought a compromise solution. The senior partners were willing to demote Ehrman but not allow one of their contemporaries to take control. They compromised on a new partner whom they hardly knew and who had recently joined the firm from the Nixon administration: Peter G. Peterson, former Commerce Secretary. This proved to be a mixed blessing in the long run but solved a serious management problem affecting the immediate future of Lehman.

I was happy with the solution. Something had to be done for the business to survive. My backers, Glanville and Glucksman, had stepped up and used their power to remove Ehrman. Later, I came to learn there was no free lunch.

My bet was the economy would recover and Lehman with it. That proved correct even though it took a few years to start seeing the transition. The mid-70s were dead space as far as investment banking was concerned. However, some good happened.

In 1973, at the height of the energy crisis, the firm sent George W. Ball and me to the Middle East to determine if there was potential business for Lehman in that rapidly changing region. George Ball had been Under Secretary of State for John F. Kennedy and Lyndon Johnson, and we had worked together on the DC-10 financing at McDonnell Douglas. He was highly respected worldwide and a great guy. It was a gift for me to travel the world with him and meet the incredible people who were happy to see him. He and I were tight and could talk about anything. He loved to hear my experiences as a Marine, and we had many discussions about Vietnam. He was the lone voice in President Johnson's cabinet speaking against the war, and as I came to oppose the war in retrospect, I developed great regard for his courage.

George arranged meetings with senior government representatives in Lebanon and Kuwait, and I continued to Abu Dhabi on my own. We concluded it was premature for Lehman to establish a presence in the region, and the firm took no action. We were right, as to this day, no US banking firm has a measurable presence in the region.

CONAGRA

In 1974, I received a phone call from Mike Harper. He had become CEO of ConAgra, an Omaha-based company about which I knew nothing. ConAgra was in three businesses: animal feed distribution, flour milling, and poultry production. The company had $160 million in debt, lost $14 million the prior year, and had a New York Stock Exchange market value of $10 million. Just short of bankruptcy, in my opinion. Mike said he needed help. He wanted to sell a Puerto Rican subsidiary to raise the capital necessary for the company to survive. I'd had a good experience with Mike on the

Pillsbury deal but had become a Lehman partner only a few months before he called and was sensitive about taking on a client with ConAgra's financial profile. I explained, and notwithstanding ConAgra's dicey financial situation, asked if he would send a $25,000 retainer to solve my problem at Lehman. He did so without hesitation, and I went to work immediately with great appreciation for his understanding.

Within a couple of months, I had negotiated a contract for the sale of the Puerto Rican business to Continental Grain Company, a major private company with no financial problems and no worries about stock analysts' opinions. Mike called one day and told me the ConAgra business had turned positive, and he decided to keep the Puerto Rican subsidiary as the need to sell it had passed. He told me ConAgra was going to pay my full fee as if the business had been sold. You can imagine what it meant to me as a brand-new partner who had worked for weeks to secure a good result for ConAgra. I can't recall the exact amount of the fee—maybe $100,000 including the retainer—but what mattered was the mutual trust and appreciation Mike and I established. We worked together for the next fifteen years, building ConAgra into a major company. When Mike retired, the total market valuation of ConAgra was $15 billion. Mike and I became good friends, and this elevated the satisfaction of working as partners. To think it all started with a phone call from Hal Dean to Bill Spoor and a $20 million chicken deal still makes me smile.

THE BUSINESS OF MERGERS AND ACQUISITIONS

I became more interested in M&A in the mid-1970s when Morgan Stanley and Goldman Sachs created specialized M&A departments. They explained to clients that their specialists worked on nothing but M&A, while competitors utilized corporate coverage people with little to no M&A experience. This was the absolute truth.

I had met Marty Lipton a few times, and in 1975, I called and asked to see him. Marty Lipton and Joe Flom were already business icons. Each had founded his law firm with a few partners, and Wachtell, Lipton, Rosen & Katz and Skadden, Arps, Slate, Meagher & Flom had quickly achieved resounding success. They, without question, were the leading law firms in the rapidly developing world of M&A.

I explained to Marty my vision for how M&A could become more active and how CEOs could employ it more aggressively. I asked Marty if he would teach me the finer points of the business. I told him Lehman was unprepared to compete with Morgan and Goldman's specialized operations, which, in my opinion, posed a serious threat to Lehman's future. Marty said he'd be delighted to help and suggested we meet every Saturday morning at 9 a.m. at his office in New York. We did that for many weeks, and I learned from the master and his partner Erica Steinberger (also his wife at the time) the finer points of M&A. Lehman became an important client, and Marty and I have remained very close friends throughout the years.

Whenever I needed advice, I talked to Marty or his most senior partner Ed Herlihy, and no one else. I got to know Ed when Marty asked me to help him join a golf club. Ed and I immediately connected and became close friends and golf partners. Ed's business advice has always been right on the mark over our many years of collaboration, and our friendship is invaluable. How lucky I was when Marty decided to help a young Lehman partner learn about M&A.

At Lehman in the mid-1970s, the partner responsible for a client company would be the first to know if a potential M&A assignment might be developing. The partner would work on the matter regardless of whether he had M&A experience or the personal characteristics required for success. Sometimes the weakest partner in the firm would find himself at the helm of a complicated situation, perhaps opposite Morgan Stanley or Goldman Sachs, and quickly learn he was in charge of a disaster. By the time he called for help, if he did, it was almost always too late to salvage the business situation and, in some cases, too late to preserve the client relationship.

It was clear to me Lehman could not continue successfully without setting up a dedicated M&A business to meet the competition. Every dollar of my net worth was tied up in

Lehman capital, which made it imperative that something be done. I felt confident I was well suited to create and run a specialized M&A operation and bring Lehman into the modern world of this lucrative business.

I explained my rationale to Glucksman and Peterson. Glucksman got it, as he always did, and told me if I thought it was a good idea, I could count on his support. Peterson didn't quite connect the dots and thought I intended to set up a statistical department to supply M&A analysis to other partners. I was flabbergasted since this was the exact opposite of what I explained was required, but I decided to let a sleeping dog lie and go about my business as planned, as he was not opposed to what he thought I was going to do.

Right around that time, a black-tie partners' dinner had been scheduled to build morale since the firm was doing well again, and the dismal mid-70s period had come to an end. I sat next to Steve Bershad, a friend and partner whom I respected, and explained what I was about to do. Steve was aghast. He said I was crazy, and it would never work because no one would cooperate with me, given the Lehman culture. I was giving up the firm's premier group of clients for the opportunity to fall on my sword, and I must reconsider immediately.

I couldn't quarrel with any of Steve's points, but I moved onward without hesitation. I believed in two critical assumptions that trumped all the negatives. First, M&A was going to become a huge business because American CEOs were aggressive and were going to act accordingly to develop their businesses using M&A as it had never been used before. Second, if we didn't act, Lehman's most important clients would migrate to the firms with specialized M&A groups with superior skills. M&A is an area of corporate competition where losing is not an option for a CEO. If Lehman did not create a competent, dedicated M&A group, the firm would decline, and my net worth and that of the partners would shrink substantially.

I recruited a young associate, Steve Waters, and a younger analyst, Conrad Meyer, to help establish Lehman's M&A Department in 1977. Morgan Stanley and Goldman Sachs were miles ahead. However, the corporate world was vast, and there were many companies to approach. Things happen quickly in the financial world, and performances can build reputations rapidly. Sadly, we almost immediately encountered a discouraging setback, an "own goal" in soccer parlance.

Eaton Corporation was a Cleveland-based company we began calling on even though there was no prior relationship with our firm. We developed acquisition ideas, and one got their attention. Carborundum Corporation was a perfect fit for Eaton, and its stock was trading at an all-time low, making it attractive for acquisition. Its balance sheet was solid, and the business was well managed—its only problem was a languishing stock price. Eaton could afford to buy Carborundum for cash through a tender offer for all of its shares. We advised Eaton they needed to pay a substantial premium over Carborundum's current stock price because other companies would step in if our pricing was too low, and Carborundum would agree to a deal with one of them. Even with an aggressive premium, all the financial numbers worked for Eaton. But then our luck ran out.

Word got to Peterson we were getting close to announcing a major deal. He was distantly acquainted with Eaton's chairman and insisted we involve him. We did not need his help, but it was impossible to tell the head of our firm he couldn't participate. We went to Cleveland to discuss the proposed transaction with the CEO of Eaton, and without prior warning, Peterson offered to attend Eaton's board meeting to evaluate the deal. Neither I nor my team were invited. At the board meeting, Peterson, with little comprehension of the facts or M&A tactics, overruled our advice on the size of the premium and told the Eaton directors it could be cut in half. The board took his advice—after all, how could they disagree with the head of Lehman Brothers—and dispatched a letter from Eaton's CEO to the Carborundum board of directors seeking a meeting to discuss Eaton's planned "friendly tender offer."[11] Within days, Kennecott Copper and Carbo-

---

11   Offer letter sent to target company's board saying we'd like this to be a negotiated acquisition but we are prepared to make a unilateral tender offer if necessary.

rundum announced a merger at the price we had originally told Eaton was necessary to clear the market. Peterson's disastrous interference cost us a large fee and an opportunity to demonstrate our competence in the world of big-time M&A. Worst of all, we were humiliated throughout the business world as Morgan Stanley, who represented Kennecott, wasted no time in sending the story around to their clients and prospective clients. They asserted that Lehman partners were dangerous amateurs who shouldn't be considered for even the most rudimentary M&A situations.

We took a beating, but our small group did not give up. With hard work and a rapidly growing M&A market, we caught up with Morgan Stanley and Goldman Sachs in a little over two years and established ourselves as one of the top M&A practitioners. One of the deals which helped us earn our reputation was famously complex: the Pac-Man defense.[12]

PAC-MAN

In late 1977, Lehman acquired Kuhn, Loeb & Co., an old-line firm that had lost its way because it was extremely conservative and risk-averse and had not coped with the dynamic changes to Wall Street in the late 1970s. Kuhn Loeb was not making much money at the time but had two valuable assets that did not appear on its financial statements: some

---

12 A hostile takeover defense strategy in which the target bids to acquire the hostile bidder who made the first unsolicited offer.

impressive, long-term client relationships and a small group of excellent bankers who could be successful at a more aggressive firm like Lehman Brothers.

When Lehman acquired Kuhn Loeb, the Kuhn Loeb partners received only 13 percent of the equity in the combined firm, which was named Lehman Brothers Kuhn Loeb. Before long, unsurprisingly, the name was changed back to Lehman Brothers. One of the most productive former Kuhn Loeb partners was William Kearns. Bill Kearns is an amazing salesman. He understood what the deal was about, was fearless about asking for the order, and was incredibly likable. The instinct buried deeply in his persona was how to put those qualities together and get hired in a wide variety of situations. "Billy Boy" (as he was called by Ed Hennessy, CEO of Allied Corporation) and I were a match made in heaven.

In 1982, the Bendix Corporation made an unsolicited tender offer for Martin Marietta, a major defense contractor that was much larger than Bendix. Martin Marietta almost immediately made a counter cash tender for Bendix, creating the famous "Pac-Man defense." Bendix bought a 44 percent equity position in Martin, who bought a similarly sized position in Bendix. That is where Pac-Man stopped. Bendix needed a "friendly back-end merger"[13] to acquire 100 percent

13 Retires remaining shares of common stock at end of contested takeover, thus allowing cash flows to be controlled by acquiring company—often required by bank lenders before financing remainder of a transaction.

of Martin, and Martin did not want to acquire the remainder of Bendix, having created Pac-Man strictly to stop Bendix in its tracks. Bendix had assumed once they owned a large position in Martin stock, Martin would capitulate and negotiate a "friendly" back-end to the deal. They never anticipated the show-stopping Pac-Man defense that Martin deployed.

Enter Bill Kearns and his relationship with Ed Hennessy. Ed Hennessy was the aggressive CEO of Allied Corporation, who would push hard to develop his business, exactly the type envisioned when I founded the M&A business at Lehman. Allied was a substantial corporation with defense businesses that would blend well with Bendix.

Bill was acquainted socially with Ed as both lived in suburban New Jersey, where Allied was headquartered. He was aware Hennessy was very interested in acquiring Bendix and set a meeting for the three of us. I explained how I thought the situation could be advanced with Bendix, and Ed hired us on the spot.

The CEO of Bendix was Bill Agee, a forty-four-year-old who had divorced his wife and became romantically involved with an attractive blond in her late twenties named Mary Cunningham. Mary was Agee's head of corporate development at Bendix. Mary would be a prominent player in the developments to come. "Me Too" was not even a figment of anyone's imagination back then.

Agee was stuck. He owned 44 percent of Martin Marietta, but the banks would not lend more money unless Bendix was assured of acquiring 100 percent control, which was why they needed a "friendly" deal to buy the remainder of Martin's common stock. If Martin Marietta bought control of Bendix, which they could easily afford, Agee's shelf life would be measured in hours. He was hanging by a thread because Martin did not want to acquire Bendix, whose businesses they were not interested in.

We worked on the financial analysis, which showed Allied could raise enough cash to acquire control but would also need a friendly stock merger to achieve a 100 percent acquisition. That meant we had to make a deal with Agee (and his girlfriend) that preserved his ego and his perceived position as a major figure in US business. Hennessy was intensely Catholic and had been educated in Jesuit schools. He thought Agee was a fool for allowing Bendix to become trapped in its current business impasse and found the situation bizarre, especially given Agee's romantic activities.

Agee was willing to meet, so we set a time at the Helmsley Palace Hotel on Madison Avenue. Ed and I walked into a large suite, and Agee and Cunningham were sitting on a couch holding hands! Ed could hardly speak. I explained how we wanted to proceed and how the deal would unfold. We didn't have all the facts because United Technologies Corporation, a much larger company than the other three participants, had joined the fray. We assumed United Technologies might buy stock in Martin Marietta to help them completely block Bendix.

Ed asked me, "What am I going to do with this guy?"

Without hesitation, I said, "You are going to make him president of the new company. That's how we get our friendly merger. Later, you can do whatever you want."

Ed's eyes glazed, but he nodded in agreement. Agee agreed to the deal because he knew neither Martin nor UTC would allow such a face-saving gesture.

The following afternoon, the Allied board met in New York and approved the acquisition of Bendix, which included 44 percent of Martin Marietta's stock. I suggested Ed, Joe Flom, and I immediately go to Washington and meet with the top management of Martin to explain our deal. Paul Thayer, Chairman of LTV[14] and a board member of both Martin Marietta and Allied, volunteered to set up the meeting and fly us down to Washington on his plane. After he arranged the meeting, he said he had to make one more phone call which, in retrospect, was disastrous.

We met with Martin's CEO Tom Pownall, and other members of top management at their Bethesda headquarters

---

14   Ling-Temco-Vought was a large conglomerate in aerospace and other businesses.

that evening. Pownall was very impressive, a man of significant presence. He said to Ed, "Look, you own 44 percent of us, go ahead and acquire the rest and combine the three companies if you want." Ed and I went to a small conference room and discussed alternatives. I suggested as strongly as I could that he should seize the opportunity to acquire Martin, an undeniably outstanding company that could be worked into the overall transaction without triggering antitrust considerations. Ed chose not to because of the amount of debt that would be incurred. Instead, we negotiated a standstill agreement allowing Allied to continue to own 44 percent of Martin stock without buying more. Martin's stock doubled in value in months, and Allied sold it back to Martin for a significant profit. Too bad Ed felt risk-averse that night. The three-way merger was a once-in-a-lifetime opportunity.

Paul Thayer was a leading member of the US aerospace top management echelon. He served as Assistant Secretary of Defense and was a man of outstanding background and achievement. Unfortunately, the call he made as we were leaving for Bethesda was to his girlfriend in Dallas (he was married), who was a stockbroker. Thayer told her what had just transpired at the board meeting, and she bought Bendix stock before the news was released to the press. Thayer was sentenced to four years in prison for obstructing justice in the insider trading case that followed. It was a harsh sentence because prosecutors were making an example of a prominent person to show that insider trading would not be tolerated.

Agee and Cunningham invited a *Fortune* magazine reporter to accompany them on the Allied plane back to Detroit, along with a photographer to capture the whole story in glossy PR. Ed Hennessy was a decisive CEO with a very short fuse. Predictably, the Hennessy-Agee management team lasted less than a month. Bill and Mary married and moved to Idaho and into obscurity.

PERSONAL LIFE

—

LEHMAN BROTHERS HAD A TRADITION OF INVITING ALL employees to a Christmas party. The secretaries from Brooklyn showed up in formal dresses, and the men wore suits. There was a band, people danced, the consumption of food and alcohol was legendary, and since this was long before the "Me Too" movement, aggressive behavior was not always avoided.

The partners were seated at various tables arranged by staff who had responsibility for all things related to the party. At the 1976 party in mid-December, I found myself seated next to Anne Gilchrist, an attractive, extremely bright twenty-seven-year-old analyst in corporate finance, one of only a few women working as banking professionals at the firm. We got up to dance, and while we were dancing, she said, "Well, you're the perfect size." She told me later that she had asked to be seated next to me as she was friendly with the woman in charge of the party.

Annie had no idea my marriage had cooled as my career had taken off. I was off-balance as the two most important parts of my life were going in opposite directions. After getting to know one another at the party, we started to see more of each other than before. Nothing happened for a while until things changed. We were married for twenty-seven years, had three children, and achieved many mutual and individual accomplishments. Jay was born on October 31, 1984, and Patsy and Willy on February 2, 1990. In addition to being an outstanding mother, Annie was a devoted stepmother to my three older children with Susan. All three continue to maintain their relationships with her.

CHANGES AT LEHMAN

———

LEW GLUCKSMAN SURVIVED HIS ALMOST FATAL NEGA-
tive carry position, and so did Lehman Brothers. Glucksman's
power came from his complete control of Lehman's fixed-income business. He added bond trading and underwriting,
mortgage trading, real estate financing, leasing, and other
activities related to debt and fixed-income securities to the
commercial paper business he founded. He despised Peterson, who treated him like a subordinate rather than a partner.
But deep down, Lew was insecure about his ability to deal
with CEOs. Managing the fixed-income business did not
require him to interface with them. Investment banking was
Lehman's heritage and its most profitable business activity,
and if getting rid of Peterson hurt banking, doing so would
backfire on Glucksman. So in 1982, unable to contain his
frustration any longer, he confronted Peterson and insisted
they become co-CEOs. After a lot of hemming and hawing,
Peterson acquiesced, figuring it was his least worst option.
He did not want to have a banking vs. fixed-income war,
which would damage the firm at a time when business was

going well. Nothing changed on the surface, but the script was written for what would become the final act between these two characters.

Around this time, my great friend Chas Phillips had moved from Salomon Brothers to Morgan Stanley, where he had flourished. His intellect and easy wit had earned him great popularity within the firm. He was currently in an important and prestigious job as secretary to the management committee which ran the firm. He was, in effect, the adjutant to Morgan Stanley's general staff.

In the spring of 1983, Chas called and suggested I become a member of the prestigious National Golf Links of America in Southampton. He said he worked for two men on Morgan Stanley's management committee who had grown up playing at the National, and he would like to arrange a game for the four of us. The following weekend we played on a beautiful morning in May with Parker Gilbert and Bill Black. My game rose to the occasion, and I shot a one under par 72. About six weeks later, I received my first bill from the National.

The clubhouse and the golf course at National are legendary and spectacularly beautiful. But what developed because of Chas' thoughtfulness and friendship was far more significant than the pleasure of being a member of a great golf club. Bill Black and I became good friends and played golf almost every weekend that summer. I also got to know Parker quite well. These relationships converged after Labor Day in 1983.

In July that same year, Glucksman, emboldened by his power move to become co-CEO, dropped the hammer on Peterson once again. He told Peterson that he had to leave the firm because it had become impossible for them to work together. Peterson was a controversial leader for many reasons and felt he did not have enough support to mount a successful counterattack against Glucksman. Rather than embarrass himself in an odds-against situation and tarnish his public persona, he quickly resigned and declared victory on his way out the door.

Glucksman had called Peterson's card, and it had worked. I was as bullish about Lehman's prospects as I had ever been. Lehman finally had an opportunity to build a culture based on honesty, transparency, and performance. Unfortunately, the honeymoon was brutally short.

Lehman was on a September fiscal year and paid employees' year-end bonuses in late September. Ninety percent of most employees' compensation was paid through the bonus. This was Glucksman's first time controlling the bonus payout, which would also be an indication of his leadership philosophy.

The firm had moved from the historic and inefficient One

William St. building to a modern skyscraper at 55 Water Street. The entire investment banking division was housed on a single floor, which proved remarkably synergistic. People interacted with each other, discussed their business activities and, began to exchange ideas and suggestions. About a week after the bonus distribution, I was walking around the floor. I passed by my friend Peter Solomon's office, and since the door was open, I walked in. Peter was pacing around and seemed agitated. What he proceeded to tell me changed the rest of my life.

Peter said he couldn't get over what Glucksman had done with the firm's year-end bonus pool. Business in 1983 had been good, and the pool contained many millions of dollars. The firm had a defunct executive committee of which Peter was a member. Peter told me that Glucksman had called a meeting of that committee supposedly to discuss how to allocate the bonuses. Glucksman proposed a bonus distribution list allocating 40 percent of the pool to himself and three of his fixed-income managers. This was a highly disproportionate amount, which disadvantaged investment bankers and other employees dependent on receiving the vast majority of their annual income from the pool. Glucksman didn't ask for the committee's opinion, just their approval. Most of the members spoke up and said this was a mistake for numerous reasons. Then came the ultimate insult: Peter said Glucksman approached each member of the committee, offering to increase their bonus by $100,000 if they consented to the payout. However, when he got to Peter, he made the offer for consent but with only a $25,000 bump to his bonus. Peter was crazed. He said, "He only offered me a tip!"

I instantly knew my values were at odds with Lehman's, and I should leave the firm. If I didn't, I would lose my self-respect. I had been at Lehman for my entire career, almost sixteen years, and had been a partner for almost eleven. My net worth was fully invested in Lehman equity.

I needed to determine where I might go and quickly decided I would join Morgan Stanley if they were interested. I knew Bill Black and Parker Gilbert, who were members of the committee running the firm, and I liked and respected them. Goldman Sachs was my other potential option, but I didn't know their top people as well. I had a good relationship with Bob Greenhill at Morgan Stanley going back to the deal with Nestlé years before. Greenhill had built Morgan's M&A business from scratch as I had done at Lehman. He had recently promoted himself to lead the investment banking department.

MORGAN STANLEY
1983–1990

I PICKED UP THE PHONE AND CALLED BILL BLACK AND explained I wanted to have lunch to discuss an important matter. We decided to play golf at National that Saturday and have lunch afterward. We sat out on the screened-in dining porch overlooking the Peconic Bay. The menu at National had not changed in seventy-five years—cold lobster with mustard sauce, clam broth, local fish cakes, creamed corn, and macaroni and cheese. Rice cakes for dessert.

I told my story to Bill, and he reacted unemotionally. He said I should approach Greenhill, whose support I would need if this was going to work. He thought Greenhill had a favorable opinion of me, and it probably came down to whether Bob thought it made sense or not. He and Parker would support me if Bob wanted to bring me in.

I called Greenhill first thing Monday morning and told him

I had decided to leave Lehman and would like to come and talk to him about joining Morgan Stanley. He suggested we meet at 4 p.m. at his office. I explained my reasons for leaving and told Bob I thought his choice of a successor as head of M&A was not optimal and explained why. He was noncommittal about that subject but did not seem to be put off by my candor. When we finished our discussion, he said without hesitation, "We need to get this done. Morgan Stanley is the right place for you."

Bob told me I would be only the third partner Morgan Stanley had brought in from outside the firm. The other two had agreed to a 1 percent partnership interest. I told him I owned 2 percent of Lehman. I was impressed with how directly he dealt with that sensitive point. He said, "If you push the executive committee, they will reluctantly agree to 2 percent." Bob suggested I agree to 1 percent, and if I performed the way he was sure I would, I would be way ahead in terms of ownership and compensation as time went on. I took his advice and never regretted that decision. I knew Morgan Stanley was where I wanted to be, and that was more important than the difference between one and two percent. I was treated extremely well the entire time I was there. Bob and I were always direct with one another, and I respect and admire how he handled himself.

My first day as a partner of Morgan Stanley was October 23, 1983. My decision to leave Lehman and the transition to

Morgan Stanley transpired in a few weeks. Sad to say, within a little more than a year, Glucksman's reign at Lehman produced major business and morale problems, and the firm was hastily acquired by American Express for a distressed price. An era had come to an unfortunate end.

Lehman had an abundance of talented individuals immersed in a combative culture with almost no teamwork. Years before, at a cocktail party at Bruce Wasserstein's East Hampton estate, Bruce, Steve Schwarzman, and I were standing together having a drink and Bruce said, "I like both of you guys, and I can't understand why people at Lehman hate each other." Without hesitation, Steve said, "Bruce, if you were at Lehman, we'd hate you too!"

Morgan Stanley did not have many individual stars. Greenhill was a star, and that slightly distanced him from his peers at the top of the firm, even though, without his leadership, their M&A business would have lagged behind the competition. Morgan had a roster of high-achieving people who thrived by functioning as a team, the opposite of Lehman's eat-what-you-kill approach. Each culture had pluses and minuses, but overall the Morgan system was far superior. My experience as a Marine taught me the value of teamwork, but at the same time, I wasn't afraid to take significant risks when doing so seemed worthwhile. Blending these characteristics resulted in success for Morgan Stanley and me in the intensive period of M&A, which transpired during the latter half of the 1980s.

A few weeks after joining Morgan Stanley, I took on a small assignment. Milton Bradley, a toy manufacturer, was being greenmailed by aggressive investors.[15] Ronald Perelman, a successful financial entrepreneur, had assembled a 4.9 percent stake and disclosed his possible intention to acquire the company. Two other investors had done the same. This caused the Milton Bradley stock price to soar, putting management under pressure to take action: either try and greenmail (buy out) the investors at prices that would exceed current market values or agree to put the company up for sale. Management, who owned a substantial amount of stock, wanted to sell.

We discussed valuation and concluded the business was worth around $300 million. I decided to negotiate an incentive fee.[16] If the shareholders received $300 million or less, Morgan Stanley would receive substantially less than a normal fee. But, if I made a deal for more than $300 million, Morgan Stanley would get 10 percent of everything over that amount. Management and its board were pleased with the arrangement. Hasbro acquired Milton Bradley for $350 million, and Morgan Stanley received a $6.5 million

---

15   When an investor buys stock and threatens a takeover to pressure the target to repurchase the stock at a higher price.

16   A fee based on performance compared to an agreed benchmark.

fee, far more than normal. It was a small transaction, but in those days, a $6.5 million fee was notable, and my creative approach put me on the map at Morgan Stanley.

Morgan Stanley was extremely homogeneous. Most of the senior partners had graduated from Harvard, Yale, or Princeton. Bill Black, Parker Gilbert, and Bob Greenhill went to Yale. People wore the same style of clear eyeglass frames, and many of the men wore suspenders, probably because Greenhill did. There seemed to be an unspoken desire for maximum homogeneity, which, in my opinion, hindered creativity and aggressive thought and action, the very characteristics needed most to succeed in M&A and business in general. I had no conscious plan to try and make the big ship make a slow turn out at sea but knew I must be myself and do business the way I always had.

As 1984 progressed, I became busy pursuing new business and working on numerous transactions. Wall Street was a dynamic universe—a financial cauldron of ideas, trading strategies, and corporate advice affecting billions of dollars and the financial security of millions of people. It was virtually impossible to plan five years ahead because the changes could be dramatic and unpredictable. A firm with a static and structured environment could easily fall behind and never recover its former position in the hierarchy of Wall Street.

In June 1984, Greenhill told me he was going to make me

head of M&A. It was a total surprise as I had not discussed the possibility with Bob or anyone else. I made some changes shortly after taking over the department on July 1. One involved a Monday morning meeting where all members of the M&A department gathered in the firm's large board room and "reviewed" all active assignments. The most junior member of each team recited the review using code names for which there was no index for security reasons. My impression was that few people understood what was being presented and, of course, were too intimidated to ask for help. The meeting started at 8 a.m. and often ran until 1 p.m. I decided this was a waste of time, effort, and money. I discontinued the meeting, a popular decision.

Within the M&A department, a group of ten professionals plus support staff called TDG—the Transaction Development Group—was led by an extremely talented and creative partner named Bob Lessin. Greenhill had formed this group to develop acquisition ideas for Morgan's most important clients. Even if an idea was rejected, it provided a reason to talk to the client, and other business often evolved from those discussions.

Bob Lessin was particularly enthusiastic about McGraw Edison, a potential acquisition he had identified for Cooper Industries, an industrial conglomerate based in Houston. He had proposed it to his contact in corporate development, who rejected it out of hand. He told Bob that Cooper had looked at it before, and it didn't interest them. Lessin told me Cooper was not up to date on the McGraw situation, and there had been changes that made McGraw an excellent fit with Cooper. I knew Bob Cizik, CEO of Cooper, who was approachable and knew how to make deals. Bob Lessin was very smart, and his strong opinion that McGraw Edison was worth Cooper's consideration was enough for me.

I called Cizik, and he repeated what his corporate development person had told Lessin. I said, "Bob, tell you what, let me come to Houston and explain why we like this idea so much and what has changed at McGraw since you looked at it—after all, it's my nickel; it costs you nothing for me to come and see you." He laughed, and we made a date.

We had an excellent meeting in Houston. Lessin was impressive and proved he was right that McGraw Edison was a fit for Cooper. Cizik was interested, and we agreed to take a thorough look at the potential acquisition. About a week later, there was a story in the press indicating McGraw Edison and Forstmann Little were in discussions about a leveraged buyout of McGraw. The transaction had not been contractually agreed, so the announcement must have been prompted by a leak. Cizik seized the opportunity and, within a few days, bid a higher price, all in cash. Forstmann dropped out, and Cooper completed the acquisition. Forstmann was also on the other side of the Revlon transaction discussed later in this book. Years later, Forstmann hired Gleacher

& Company to help them buy International Management Group (IMG), the global sports and talent management business they developed into a very profitable leveraged investment.

MILKEN AND DREXEL

During the latter half of the 1980s, many large and controversial M&A transactions were initiated by Mike Milken and his high-yield junk bond[17] operation at Drexel Burnham Lambert, known forever after as Drexel. Milken was a savant who realized that defaults in the universe of lower credit-rated bonds were substantially less frequent than perceived by the market. Therein lay the opportunity. One could invest in these mispriced securities and make very attractive returns without undue risk. Companies could issue high-yield debt in large amounts in a market hungry for more supply. Milken and his traders at Drexel had given birth to a huge new "junk bond" market, which had implications for much more than trading and investment.

Many companies rated by Moody's and Standard & Poor's (S&P) as less than investment grade took advantage of a buoyant market to refinance existing debt, invest in new projects, and acquire other companies. Milken soon realized he could use high-yield financing to make unsolicited take-

---

17 Corporate debt securities rated less than investment grade, i.e., too risky for prudent investment.

over bids for major companies almost without regard for their size and market value. He recruited financial entrepreneurs such as Ronald Perelman, Carl Icahn, Sam Heyman, and others, providing them with sizable pools of capital with no restrictions on how it could be used. They didn't hesitate to put it into play. Perelman went after Revlon, Icahn went after Texaco, Heyman went after Union Carbide, KKR[18] went after RJR Nabisco, and Perelman then went after Gillette, all between 1985 and 1989. This caused the restructuring of American business. Companies knew that if they needed belt-tightening, they'd best do it themselves because if they didn't, Milken might support a hostile takeover financed with junk-bond debt orchestrated by a financial entrepreneur—a fate almost equivalent to death for most CEO members of the business roundtable.

Morgan Stanley and I represented all the targets in the list above with the exception of the RJR Nabisco deal, in which we represented KKR. All the target companies remained independent, and KKR acquired RJR.

The latter half of the 1980s was the world series of M&A, and no period since has superseded that era. Working on these premier, highly visible transactions solidified my reputation, which enabled me to establish my own independent firm in 1990. Everything worked because I had the support of Morgan Stanley and my M&A teams and the confidence to

18   A private equity firm founded by Henry Kravis, George Roberts, and Jerome Kohlberg.

trust my instincts and persuade clients to follow my advice. I had the energy and motivation to engage 24/7 and block out all else in my pursuit of winning these contests. It was like playing a sport with a lot at stake. I loved it. When Milken and I met for the first time at his office on Rodeo Drive in Los Angeles, the first thing he said was, "I'm so depressed; you're so young!" I was flattered; every time we had faced each other, his bid had failed, and he was lamenting the fact I'd be around for a long time.

MAJOR M&A DEALS
OF THE 1980S

REVLON

The Revlon deal began to take shape in the spring of 1985. Revlon was founded by Charles Revson and grew into one of the most successful retailers of women's cosmetics in the world. In the late 1960s, Revson, who had long been interested in healthcare, acquired a laboratory testing company called Technicon, which became a major success. Over subsequent years Revlon acquired three other healthcare businesses. By 1984, Revlon had become a healthcare conglomerate with a mature cosmetics company attached. Its structure confused the market, and it traded for less than its theoretical sum-of-the-parts[19] valuation.

Revlon's CEO in 1985 was Michel Bergerac, a Frenchman with a gun rack over his seat on Revlon's G5, which displayed

---

19 Calculating the total value of the subsidiaries of a holding company.

a high caliber hunting rifle. Bergerac succeeded Revson as CEO in 1975 after Revson's death. He became increasingly frustrated with Revlon's stock price because even as corporate earnings grew, the common stock traded lower.

Bergerac was one of the most egotistical individuals I've encountered. He decided, as did Ross Johnson four years later at RJR Nabisco, that if the world did not appreciate the value of his company, management should buy it and reap the spoils themselves. Rather than hire an investment banker, Bergerac must have concluded that only he could figure out how to make this happen. He began to meet personally with potential buyers of the various healthcare subsidiaries. His visits were meant to stimulate interest in and establish a valuation of the businesses. Proceeds from the sales would finance management's purchase of the company. Since management was charged with running the company for the benefit of shareholders, customers, and employees and not for the potential financial gain of management itself, these visits caused confusion among potential buyers. Two were Morgan Stanley clients who came to the firm asking for advice about what was going on and what they should do.

Those visits caused me to focus on what might happen in this unorthodox situation. I worked with Conrad Meyer, a long-standing colleague and extremely bright banker who had helped me establish the M&A group at Lehman. I was sure

Bergerac would create action, but not the type he imagined. All the potential buyers would talk to investment bankers, who would sense that a number of transactions were likely to evolve. A successful bid for Revlon was probable, but it would not be conducted by Bergerac and his management team. Conrad's analysis indicated that if all the healthcare subsidiaries were marketed effectively, the proceeds would allow the buyer to own the cosmetics business for free, after all expenses. We had to move quickly, because someone was going to try and take control of this attractive opportunity.

I selected the right person, Ronald Perelman, who was not a stereotypical Morgan client. Perelman was a financial entrepreneur and the 100 percent owner of his private holding company. He was smart, honest, and very aggressive. Conrad and I explained the opportunity, and the pièce de résistance was our assertion that he could own the iconic Revlon cosmetics business for free. After a vigorous negotiation, we ended up with the following structure: Perelman would bid for 100 percent of Revlon, and we would initiate discussions with potential buyers of the healthcare businesses. If he acquired Revlon and we sold the healthcare businesses and created the cosmetics business "for free" as we asserted, Perelman would pay Morgan Stanley a fee of $30 million. This was a fee level Wall Street had not seen before.

I explained the situation to the Morgan Stanley management committee, and they took a deep breath. They were intrigued and agreed that someone was going to take advantage of Bergerac's naivety. But Ronald Perelman was a stretch, and I was the only one who had met him. They loved the thought of making $30 million and were reluctant to say no to me, as the M&A business was the premier business of the firm, but coming to terms with backing a financial entrepreneur going against the management of a major US company was difficult for Morgan Stanley. I made my case with three assertions: when management tries to buy a company, the world is invited to compete; someone is going to do this deal; and finally, I was confident we could deliver what we told Perelman, which would earn Morgan Stanley a $30 million fee.

Later, Parker Gilbert, Morgan's Chairman, called me to his office. He said, "Eric, I trust you, so we are going to back your judgment and go for this deal with Perelman, but I'm counting on you not to embarrass the firm." Instantly, I realized my career was riding on this deal. My assessment of how Ronald Perelman would react under more intense pressure than he'd ever imagined would be the determining factor.

Perelman made his hostile bid in August 1985, and all hell broke loose. Bergerac was crazed that this "unknown nothing" had bid for his company, upending his fantasy belief his management group (him) was the rightful owner of Revlon. Drexel, with Milken in charge, was providing $750 million of "equity" capital, and the banks would come up with the remainder if Perelman was successful. All the major Wall

Street players were trying to find a role. Joe Flom was doing the legal work for Perelman; Marty Lipton for Revlon. Teddy Forstmann's fund was a counterbidder. Lawsuits were flying back and forth. The market was astonished Morgan Stanley was backing Perelman, especially since Milken was providing the high-yield financing. All cylinders were full speed ahead.

I was trying to squeeze in a week off in the Hamptons, but Perelman was calling every thirty minutes to see what was going on. He was nervous but would not quit until he came out on top. Finally, Forstmann withdrew in November, and Perelman acquired Revlon. Conrad Meyer and the team had contracts negotiated with the buyers of the healthcare subsidiaries, and as soon as the deal closed, those contracts were executed, and all was complete. We raised more than we had predicted, Perelman owned the iconic Revlon cosmetics business "for free," and Morgan Stanley earned $30 million. The most aggressive bet of my career evolved into a major win as my instincts and judgment about Ronald Perelman had proven correct. We had forged a respectful and lucrative business relationship, though we would one day find ourselves on opposite sides in another major transaction.

UNION CARBIDE

In the last half of the 1980s, my most frequent opponent and sometimes partner was Bruce Wasserstein at First Boston. He was exceptionally bright and gifted. I found working opposite someone so highly skilled was preferable to facing a weak adversary who might be prone to taking senseless, unpredictable actions. The bankers from Goldman Sachs were good but highly scripted and not particularly innovative.

This was an extremely volatile time in M&A and banking in general. Leon Black was Drexel's M&A leader and was also thoroughly involved with financing the deals, which was extremely lucrative for Drexel. Marty Siegel at Kidder Peabody was a talented banker but succumbed to a fatal flaw and traded information on deals with Ivan Boesky for briefcases full of cash. Both Siegel and Boesky were incarcerated. Many others went to jail as a result of their actions during the latter half of the 1980s, some of whom had worked for me—Dennis Levine and Ira Sokolow at Lehman. Milken was found guilty for various trading irregularities and paid a fine of almost a billion dollars as part of his sentencing. This period was active for M&A but bleak and disruptive for Wall Street. The corruption of some of the major players was extremely unsettling.

In early December 1985, Milken picked Sam Heyman, an obscure real estate investor from New Jersey, to be the "athlete" to bid for Union Carbide. Heyman owned a small chemical company called GAF,[20] which would make the bid of $3.5 billion all in cash. Union Carbide was a major

---

20 General Aniline and Film Corporation.

chemical company and a long-time Morgan Stanley client. The company requested I represent them, and I met with Warren Anderson, the CEO. Union Carbide's top management was an older group, most of whom had been employees of the company for their entire careers. They understood the stakes: there would be brutal cost-cutting and employee reductions if Milken and Heyman prevailed. Anderson was a talented executive, and we quickly connected, which was critical to what transpired. Sullivan & Cromwell were their very capable lawyers.

Our team of corporate finance experts ran the analysis to determine the financial limits of what the company might do on its own in response to Milken's bid. The answer was not good. The company's borrowing capacity, if maximized, still left us far short of matching a $3.5 billion bid. We did not have time to sell any businesses in the face of an all-cash offer that would be concluded in a month.

Over the years, Union Carbide had developed a number of its chemical businesses into consumer-products companies, which had succeeded in their respective markets. Three highly profitable businesses stood out: Eveready Battery, STP Lubricant, and Glad (bags). We had to find a way to raise more money to hold off GAF and Milken. We could leverage the company's assets the same as they could, but we did not have the junk bond "equity" supplied by Drexel.

I believed a plan to sell these subsidiaries would cause GAF to withdraw its offer. Since it would take months to organize the financial data and auction the businesses, we had to find a way to explain the process to the market and extract some of the proceeds in advance. My idea was to have a share buyback using cash and the right for each share of common stock to receive its pro-rata share of the eventual sale proceeds. We would disclose summary unaudited financials of the three businesses, along with Morgan Stanley's estimates of what the eventual sale proceeds would be—high, medium, and low estimates. Our shareholders could either keep their stock or tender it for the cash and their share of the proceeds from the future auctions. I believed the package would be worth around $85 per share, higher than GAF would be able to offer.

The lawyers felt this was a nonstarter because the SEC would never permit such a plan. I refused to take no for an answer as this strategy was our only hope. We went overboard disclosing every risk factor imaginable and emphasized this was an offer to our shareholders who owned the businesses which were going to be sold. It was their choice to accept the package we were putting forward, or keep their shares, or take a lower cash offer from GAF. Finally, the SEC gave the go-ahead, and our offer was heavily oversubscribed by Union Carbide shareholders. GAF withdrew, and Morgan Stanley eventually sold the three companies at the highest end of the predicted range of values. The shareholders were elated.

By January 1986, the deal was over—the entire situation had started and finished in five weeks of grueling, nonstop work by my team. We worked every day except Christmas Day until the deal was done. At the board meeting to finalize all the details, I produced a case of chilled champagne, and the directors, management, bankers, and lawyers enjoyed a well-deserved toast to a victory achieved through teamwork. A month later, *Fortune* magazine ran a story about the deal, the champagne, and me. This caused rumblings in the halls of Morgan Stanley. People were jealous, but the press will run what they feel is a good story. I didn't let it distract me and went on to the next crisis.

GILLETTE

In 1986, Ronald Perelman had purchased some shares in Gillette, only to be greenmailed unceremoniously. By the summer of 1987, he had digested the Revlon acquisition and was ready for serious action. Gillette was an iconic global business and, like Union Carbide, had older management. Gillette's common stock was trading at a low P/E ratio thanks to a lack of perceived future growth and the doldrums of the mid-August summer stock market. This state of malaise changed abruptly one day when Perelman announced a fully-financed $5 billion offer for 100 percent of Gillette's common stock. He already had purchased 9.2 million Gillette common shares.

Gillette was a Morgan Stanley client and, to my surprise,

requested my assistance in dealing with the situation. I flew up to Boston and met with senior management. I told them I wanted to make sure they were comfortable with the fact that I had represented Perelman in the acquisition of Revlon. They said they had checked me out extensively and were confident about their choice.

I went to see Perelman in New York. He reassured me he had a $5 billion financing commitment from Citibank and was not dependent on Milken for money. This was a substantial change from the Revlon deal, where he was beholden to Drexel for $750 million of high-yield "equity." Gillette had an old-line, conservative Boston management team and was clearly in trouble. Perelman had offered a substantial premium and had the money lined up, creating a scenario where management might be reluctant to deprive its shareholders of an opportunity to realize an attractive profit. Top management at Gillette had other ideas. They believed Gillette was substantially undervalued and was simply going through a period of market softness. They did not want to give the company away at the wrong time and were prepared to take financial pain and criticism if necessary. I went to work.

Bruce Wasserstein called and told me he was representing Ralston Purina, who might be interested in taking a 20 percent interest in Gillette. Ralston had indicated to its shareholders its existing businesses were not growing and was planning to use its capital to repurchase company stock and make new strategic investments. A 20 percent interest in Gillette would be attractive because Ralston could consolidate 20 percent of Gillette's net income with its own, and if Gillette was undervalued and subsequently sold, Ralston would realize a substantial profit without taking undue risk.

I explained to Perelman if another party acquired a 20 percent interest, he would be relegated to an illiquid minority equity position and would not be able to acquire control of Gillette. He could either maintain his bid and risk getting blocked or try to sell his stock back to Gillette, make a profit, and be labeled a greenmailer in the press again.

The following morning Perelman called and told me he had decided to sell his 9.2 million shares back to the company. We had a board meeting that night in Boston, and all the directors were present. They were very nervous. It became clear to me if Perelman had chosen to bid for 100 percent of the stock at the premium he had already proposed, the board would have unanimously accepted his offer, and he would have become the sole owner of Gillette for $5 billion. Following my advice, the company bought and retired his shares, and Perelman made a $43 million profit. Gillette was acquired by Proctor & Gamble in 2005 for $57 billion in stock.

TEXACO

Texaco acquired the Getty Oil Company in 1984 for $10 billion, which was only the beginning. Pennzoil, another major oil company, had negotiated an agreement in principle to buy Getty. Texaco stepped in, raised the price, and made a deal with Getty, which negated Pennzoil's prior agreement.

Pennzoil sued Texaco, claiming their memorandum of agreement with Getty was binding. Pennzoil won the lawsuit and was awarded $10.5 billion in damages in 1985. It was not until 1987 that the two companies signed a final settlement to their lawsuit, with Texaco paying out $5.5 billion to Pennzoil. Prior to its battle with Pennzoil, Texaco had been the third-largest oil company in the US. After declaring bankruptcy as the result of the $10.5 billion judgment in the lawsuit and having to reorganize after the final settlement, Texaco became a much smaller company.

Carl Icahn bought $348 million worth of Texaco stock on November 26, 1987. It was a 12 million share block owned by Robert Holmes à Court, an Australian investor who had lost over $100 million in the stock market crash on October 19, 1987. Texaco hired Morgan Stanley and requested I be put in charge of the team. This was the start of more than two years of effort to help Texaco fully regain its independence. Management's decision to acquire Getty in January 1984 had cost the company dearly.

Icahn continued to buy Texaco stock and eventually came to own 16.6 percent of the company. Texaco had 243 million shares outstanding trading in the mid-30s, indicating it was impossible for Icahn to borrow enough money to buy a controlling interest. The Texaco-Pennzoil litigation had been settled, and Texaco had reemerged from bankruptcy. All that was left, as this disastrous scenario continued to evolve, was to remove Carl Icahn from the daily life of Texaco's top management. This turned out to be as difficult as any of the preceding steps. Management created proposal after proposal and negotiated them with Icahn. The usual procedure was a dinner lasting until well after midnight resulting in a tentative agreement—only for Icahn to change his mind the next morning. A great deal of wasted time and frustration ensued. I came to the conclusion that Icahn was simply enjoying himself. He had a major American company on the hook and was in all the newspapers, relishing the prestige and notoriety.

A prior experience with Icahn had influenced my conclusion. Icahn bought a 2 percent position in AT&T equity, which was never publicly disclosed. However, it made AT&T's top management hyper-nervous. Marty Lipton and I were asked to meet with the AT&T chairman, James Olson, at their Bedminster, NJ headquarters. The first thing Olson said when we walked in the room was that he had "400 people working on this." I couldn't imagine what 400 people could possibly be doing! I told Olson the best course of action was to completely ignore Icahn because he could never finance the purchase of a significant position given the size of AT&T's

market capitalization. I further explained Icahn's interest was personal publicity; he wanted to create the impression that no company, no matter the size, was impervious to his scrutiny or reach. All AT&T had to do was do nothing, and Icahn would go away. If they put in a poison pill,[21] for example, it would only give him unwarranted credibility and publicity. Lipton supported my advice, and no one ever heard of Icahn's foray into AT&T.

Jim Kinnear, Texaco's chairman, was nearing the end of his ability to tolerate more useless iterations with Icahn. This was helpful because I was about to suggest an aggressive plan to prod Icahn to withdraw. Icahn owned 16.6 percent of Texaco's common stock, some of it acquired in the last six months. An obscure SEC rule prohibited anyone who owned more than 15 percent of a company's common stock and had purchased some or all of it in the last six months from participating in the company's stock repurchase program until six months had elapsed. It is unlikely Icahn had ever come across or was advised about this regulation. If he had, he surely would have kept his position under 15 percent.

When companies repurchase their common stock, they want to pay the market price at the time and no more. I advised Kinnear to explain to Icahn we were going to offer a very high

---

21 A defensive tactic by a target company allowing existing shareholders to buy additional shares at a substantial discount, which would heavily dilute the ownership of a hostile bidder if the acquisition was completed.

price for Texaco common stock in a corporate buyback, and he would be prohibited by the SEC from selling any of his shares into our very generous offer. This plan would create an enormous special payout for every Texaco shareholder except Icahn. However, we would be prepared to offer an alternative. We would buy his stock for $2.2 billion, giving him a $782 million profit, and pay a special dividend to all shareholders, with his share worth an additional $324 million. He took the deal, and finally, at the end of January 1989, Texaco was free of all the issues generated by the decision to overbid Pennzoil to buy Getty.

I spent two years working on the various aspects of Texaco's dilemma with David Boies and Linda Robinson. David is one of the most highly regarded lawyers in the country, and Linda is the most talented PR professional I have ever worked with. Morgan Stanley was very well compensated.

RJR NABISCO AND KKR

In 1983, Steve Rattner and I sold KTLA, a major television business in Los Angeles, for KKR. This was the first of many transactions Morgan Stanley did with KKR: Safeway, Owens Illinois, RJR Nabisco, and others.

I was alone in my office on the nineteenth floor of the Exxon building on October 20, 1988. Things were quiet for a change, and the fall weather outside was at its best. I was watching the business news on my terminal and wondering why I wasn't playing golf at the National on such a gorgeous day. A ribbon of news began to meander across my screen: "Shearson Lehman and RJR management offer $75 a share for RJR Nabisco..." It went on, but I didn't bother reading the rest. I picked up the phone and called Henry Kravis. He was in his office and came right on. "Henry, they've teed it up for you. Shearson and RJR management just announced a management buyout[22] of RJR at $75 a share. They've underpriced it by at least $20 a share. I know this company like a book, and I'm sure of it."

Henry said, "That's interesting, but we don't do hostile takeovers; it would destroy our business. Management would never let us in the door."

I did my best to explain that an offer by management to buy its own company makes them just another bidder. The RJR board would form a special committee[23] to run a bidding process and eventually select a buyer if they thought the price would be attractive to the shareholders. No potential acquirer would be considered a "hostile bidder."

Henry said, "Let's meet at 5 p.m. today and discuss it further."

---

22 An acquisition in which a company's existing managers seek to acquire all or a large part of their company—a special committee of the company's board will invite other bidders to compete.

23 A committee of directors appointed by the board to take responsibility for matters in which management is conflicted.

He was tentative, but after consulting with his cousin and co-head of KKR, George Roberts, and their legal advisors, I knew they would get comfortable with participating in the bidding process.

Before I describe what took place at the meeting, I should first explain I had a great deal of experience working with Ross Johnson, CEO of RJR, and with Henry Kravis and George Roberts. In my Lehman days, I had represented Ross when he was CEO of Standard Brands, a consumer-products company with many brand names, including Planters (peanuts). Ross was a Canadian chartered accountant with a big personality. He was great to work with because he was smart and understood business, the numbers, as well as strategy and marketing.

In 1981, Ross received a call from Bob Schaeberle, CEO of Nabisco, whom he did not know. Bob told him the Bronfman family from Canada, who owned Seagram, a major distilling company, was close to making an unsolicited bid for Nabisco. Schaeberle had no interest in that happening and asked Ross if he would consider merging Standard Brands with Nabisco, thus making the combined company too large for the Bronfmans' to acquire. Schaeberle said he was sixty-three and would retire in a year-and-a-half, at which time Ross would succeed him as CEO. Ross called and I told him the combined company would be outstanding, and it came down to social issues: could Ross and Bob work well together, and could Ross trust Bob to let go when the time came to make Ross CEO?

The pro forma for a merger of equals[24] was beautiful, a dream deal. Negotiations progressed smoothly, and we agreed on the exchange rate and other terms with Morgan Stanley. Ross called me the afternoon before the merger was to be announced and asked to meet for breakfast the next morning. We met in his dining room at Standard Brands in New York. He told me he had cold feet and wasn't going to do the deal. He was only forty-nine years old and was concerned something would go wrong between him and Bob, and his career would suffer a major setback. I couldn't argue with that possibility but suggested he consider the risk-reward balance in this situation. Never in the remainder of his career would Ross be able to build a company comparable to the combined Standard Brands-Nabisco. That made this opportunity extraordinary. One of a kind. Furthermore, Schaeberle had only eighteen months until retirement, and we would have legal protection in the merger agreement stipulating Ross would become CEO. Therefore, Ross would have to screw up mightily for Bob to supersede that agreement. All considered, the potential reward far exceeded the risk.

Ross signed the merger agreement that afternoon. The stock market loved it, and the press lauded it. Bob and Ross got on

---

24 Two companies exchange their shares without a premium for shares in a new company and merge.

so well that Bob made Ross CEO in less than a year. Home run!

In 1985, Ross received a call out of the blue from Tylee Wilson, CEO of RJR, whom he did not know. Ross called me and said, "You won't believe it, RJR wants to buy the company for $5 billion in cash! Five billion dollars!"

I said, "Ross, you are the CEO of one of the best consumer-products companies on the globe. You're still young; are you sure this is for you? You wouldn't be the CEO."

He said, "It doesn't matter because there's so much to do in these big companies."

We did the deal for $5 billion in cash, and six months later, once the directors got to know Ross, they said goodbye to Wilson, who evidently was on thin ice with his board. Ross became the CEO of RJR Nabisco!

Three years later, Ross was frustrated. The more money the company earned, the more its stock declined. The diversification RJR sought when they acquired Nabisco hadn't been sufficient to quell the distaste for the tobacco industry which had been consistently rising in the US and abroad. Given that insurmountable problem, Ross felt the company ought to be withdrawn from the public market. I told him months before I was very anti-smoking and would not be inclined to involve Morgan Stanley in a deal to buy a tobacco company. Once again, I found myself on the other side of an important deal pursued by someone who had once been a client. This would not be the last time it happened. Big-time M&A was a small world.

The five-o'clock meeting with Henry Kravis took place at KKR's offices on West 57th Street. Coincidentally, RJR's offices were located in the same building. KKR had invited Drexel (Leon Black) and Merrill Lynch (Ray Minella) for financing and Bruce Wasserstein and myself for M&A. Jeff Beck, who had worked for me at Lehman, was also present, assisting Leon Black. We were ensconced in a windowless conference room while Henry and others, including their legal counsel, were on the phone with George Roberts and his colleagues in California. The topic wasn't whether they were interested in acquiring RJR—there was no doubt about that—but whether they could compete without being tagged as hostile takeover artists. After a few hours, Henry appeared and told the group they had worked through the issues and decided to move forward with preparation for a bid.

Early the following morning, I picked up the newspapers in the foyer of my apartment and glanced at the front page of the *NY Times*. Much to my amazement, a prominent article right in the middle of the page disclosed KKR was planning a bid for RJR. This was trouble. I was sure one of the bankers had leaked this to a contact at the *Times*. The piece mentioned Drexel's involvement, but that had to be subterfuge unless the reporter got it from a second source who did not make the original call. Most likely, the caller's intent was to give a friend a scoop in exchange for undefined future reciprocation and also to lock KKR into making a bid, as not doing so after this publicity would look weak. It was impossible to identify the culprit without an investigation of the phone records. To call this disgraceful behavior would be a gross understatement. I was embarrassed and disgusted. I was sure KKR would be repulsed and had no idea how punitive their sanctions might be.

Henry Kravis was justifiably furious. However, he did not fire anyone because, at that time, the offender was undetectable. Instead, he expressed his disgust and disappointment in no uncertain terms and told us if anything like this happened again, he would fire all of us without hesitation. We were lucky he hadn't already done so.

The tone had changed between the advisor group and the principals. Mutual trust had plummeted to zero. That morning, this deal, the biggest and most publicized LBO ever, became a "zombie" deal. KKR used the valuation and pricing analysis we provided to make the initial bid but almost never consulted Bruce or me for tactical or economic advice. I had never experienced anything remotely like this during my career. It was especially disappointing since I had worked a lot with George and Henry and we were friends. Things warmed up toward the end of the deal, and our friendship continued once it was over. Eventually, after much "detective" work, KKR concluded both Bruce Wasserstein and Jeff Beck had independently leaked the information to the *Times* the night of our initial meeting.

KKR's opening bid was $90 per share. They closed out the process and claimed the prize in late November 1988 with a price of $109 per share, $25 billion in total. Between $90 and $109, most of the other prominent LBO firms made an appearance, essentially to prove their manhood. KKR was the leading private equity firm[25] at the time, and I believe they felt it imperative to prevail. It took all their considerable skill and mental acumen to untangle RJR Nabisco over the following decade, pay down the acquisition debt, and retrieve their equity. The return on their investment was nominal at best.

---

25 A pool of capital used to buy or invest in companies with maximum leverage in the capital structure - formerly called leveraged buyouts.

THE END OF AN ERA

IN DECEMBER 1988, SHORTLY AFTER THE COMPLETION
of the RJR Nabisco deal, Drexel pled guilty to criminal
counts of mail and securities fraud, removed Milken from
his position, and paid $650 million in fines. In January 1989,
the SEC filed six felony counts of mail and securities fraud
against Drexel, and in February 1990, Drexel declared bankruptcy and dissolved its business.

The era from 1983 to 1988 was one of the most active M&A
periods in history. It was assuredly the most aggressively
contested. It overlapped almost perfectly with my time at
Morgan Stanley. I was lucky. All the high profile activity elevated my reputation and made the next chapter of my career
possible. I had earned it by succeeding at a high level, but it
would not have happened without the support of Morgan
Stanley and the relationships I made there.

RJR Nabisco was the last mega-deal of the era. Drexel sank
between the waves, and no existing entity was willing to fill

the void. The major investment banks had the ability to raise money but were not about to establish "corporate raider" departments and destroy their relationships with corporate America.

Milken had accomplished something difficult and unique: he had created a vast and effective capital market. Companies and individual entrepreneurs could raise capital to deploy as they wished and traders had billions of dollars' worth of securities with complex risk factors to bet on—all the result of Milken's brilliance.

Milken and I invested separately and coincidentally in the same startup company in the late 1990s. We both lost 100 percent of our investment and had many phone conversations in the process. My conclusion was Mike is a pleasant guy with a ton of ideas, a few of which make sense and work out. His vision of the misperception of the high-yield default rate was genius, and he took it to the top of the mountain. He's had similar success over the last twenty years with his philanthropic initiatives in medical research, which have benefited millions of people around the world.

The absence of a catalyst created an eerie calm in the M&A world. Many companies in the US had restructured on their own, fearing if they didn't, someone would do it for them. M&A had become an accepted corporate business activity. Private equity firms had proliferated, and the banks were happy to pick up some of the slack Drexel's absence had left in the high-yield market. The stock market was in fine shape, and 1989 went into the books as a successful year for Morgan Stanley.

My last few weeks at Morgan Stanley were bittersweet. I had finally decided to strike out on my own and continue my M&A career without the support of a major banking firm. I had debated this possibility with myself for the past two years. I thought I could succeed, but I was happy at Morgan, which made it hard for me to pull the trigger. I had been envious two years earlier when my friend Bruce Wasserstein founded Wasserstein Perella with Joe Perella, another friend of mine. In fact, Bruce called me and said, "Why don't you join us; we'll change the name of the firm and have all the superstars under one roof." I was flattered but knew if I decided to take the risk, I wanted to do it alone: I would sink or swim on my own.

This was a clear fork in my road. I could play it safe and stay at Morgan Stanley, but I knew if I did, I would second-guess the decision for the rest of my life. My decision to go out on my own was not about making more money. I discussed the situation with my wife, Annie, who by that time was probably tired of talking about it. I told her if I left, I would possibly earn 25 percent of what I was making at Morgan Stanley. To her great credit, she replied without hesitation, "So what? Go ahead and do it." I wanted to build and manage my own firm and prove my ability to compete with the major investment banks for the most significant M&A mandates. Win or lose, I wanted to meet the challenge, and I overwhelmingly believed I had the will to win.

I met with my close friend and lawyer, Marty Lipton, and we discussed how to handle things so that until I revealed my plans, my full attention would be on Morgan Stanley business. I did not speak to corporate clients about my decision, nor did I make any attempt to solicit Morgan employees. Marty offered space at Wachtell Lipton so I would have a place to go immediately after I resigned and suggested the only sensible name for the firm was Gleacher & Company. All that was left was to wait until year-end bonuses were paid. The holidays passed into 1990, and my family and I went skiing in Colorado.

BECOMING MORGAN

ON JANUARY 11, 1990, I TOLD PARKER GILBERT I WAS leaving, and my decision had nothing to do with Morgan Stanley. I expressed my admiration for the firm and appreciation for how I had been treated and compensated. I felt fortunate to have so many friends at Morgan and knew, without a doubt, the House of Morgan would continue to excel in the future. My decision was personal, something I simply had to do.

Parker was quite reserved, made no attempt to change my mind, and wished me well. He allowed me a couple of hours to say goodbye to the people I had worked most closely with. Around noon, I walked out into the bleak January weather and over to Wachtell Lipton a few blocks away. It was quick: I said goodbye, and I was out on the street. The first thing that popped into my mind were the millions of dollars of unrealized investment returns I had given up as required by the terms of Morgan's employee investment funds. If one leaves, he or she is bought out of these investments at cost. Most were worth substantially more. Once I had worked through the remorse, I began calling clients and spoke to the press. A number of people I was close to at Morgan Stanley asked to join the new firm. A key hire was Marie Gentile, my amazing assistant, who became invaluable in future years. Marie and I have continued to work together without interruption for the past three decades. Jim Goodwin, Jeff Tepper, Bob Kitts, and Brian Hanson from Morgan Stanley and Jim Ferency from Salomon Brothers were immediately on board and were all successful and productive partners over many years.

I came in early the following morning to my new office, which was a cubical in the paralegal section of Wachtell. On my desk was a three-inch stack of unsolicited résumés which had arrived overnight via fax, along with a pile of telephone messages. Marie, Jim Goodwin, and others began to show up, and it started to feel like we were in business. Half a dozen CEOs had retained our services the day before for $250,000 a year each, providing working capital and motivation to come up with ideas for our new clientele. Mitsubishi Bank in Tokyo immediately dispatched an executive to New York, and we met and discussed a joint venture. I was wary of Japanese joint ventures, and nothing came of the meeting. Don Kempf, a lawyer from Kirkland & Ellis in Chicago, whom I did not know and who later became Morgan Stanley's general counsel, showed up with a check for a $1 million. Don wanted to retain our new firm to advise his client, Harold Simmons, who was planning a proxy contest in an attempt to gain control of Lockheed. We were sure Simmons would lose, so we turned down the assignment. We did not want our first high-profile deal to be one we had no chance of winning. Kempf and I later became good friends, and he joined our firm as a senior advisor after his tenure at Morgan Stanley.

A few weeks later, Michael Dobson, President of Morgan Grenfell in London, called to discuss the possibility of a business relationship with our firm. He came to New York, and we had a productive meeting. Morgan Grenfell was an iconic merchant banking name in London, where the Morgan empire originated. When the Glass-Steagall Act in 1933 caused US commercial banks to separate their investment banking operations, Morgan Guaranty spun off Morgan Stanley, and Morgan Grenfell became the third corner of the new House of Morgan triumvirate.

In December 1989, a few weeks before Dobson and I met, Deutsche Bank acquired Morgan Grenfell, their first foray into the Anglo banking world. Neither Deutsche nor Morgan Grenfell was capable of competing in the North American market for investment banking business. Deutsche is one of the largest banks in the world, and this deficiency had to be resolved. We were not interested in selling any of the equity in our brand-new firm, but we were interested in a partnership with a financial colossus like Deutsche.

Two weeks later, Jim Goodwin and I took an overnight flight

to London, showered in our hotel, and had lunch at Morgan Grenfell with John Craven, the Chairman, and Michael Dobson. We worked out an arrangement where Morgan Grenfell would inject $10 million of capital into Gleacher in exchange for a partnership interest in all future business we would accomplish jointly. No direct-equity ownership would be involved. The firm would be renamed Gleacher Morgan Grenfell, and it would conduct all investment banking business in North America involving clients of Deutsche and Morgan Grenfell. We had evolved from working for Morgan to becoming Morgan, and once again, the association would prove rewarding for our partners and for Morgan Grenfell.

We had many other business opportunities over the ensuing months. Some were tantalizing, and some were nonstarters. We moved with care and patience. We were not interested in becoming the largest possible firm, just the most profitable. We measured progress by the metric of profit per partner. We adhered to this philosophy for the entire twenty-three years of our business existence.

In the early weeks and months of starting our company, it became clear the world would provide opportunities because we had something to offer. As we developed our business, we also realized our firm's profile would evolve unpredictably.

I met with clients and prospective clients daily to tell them what we were doing and establish a dialog about what they wanted to accomplish with their business. I had breakfast one morning at the Links Club in New York with Cliff Robbins, then a Senior Associate of KKR. Cliff had worked for me at Morgan Stanley and was a standout member of the M&A team. Not surprisingly, he was doing well at KKR, and I wanted to keep in touch with him.

Beatrice Foods Co. came up in our conversation. KKR had acquired Beatrice in 1985 for $6 billion, the largest LBO ever at the time. Since then, KKR had sold off most of Beatrice's businesses but still retained many well-known food brands. However, Beatrice had been very aggressive with their tax accounting over the years, and buyers had been reluctant to acquire the potential future tax liabilities which would come with an asset-based purchase[26] of the food product lines. The various brands were quite valuable, and I knew ConAgra would have serious interest in acquiring the lot. There were two main issues: the potential tax liability and the value of the brands. Acquiring all of these assets would be the largest deal ConAgra had ever completed. There was no way they could pay 100 percent in cash, and KKR had never sold a portfolio company for anything other than cash. Cliff knew Mike Harper was different from most CEOs because of his exposure to ConAgra while he was at Morgan Stanley. Mike

---

26 When an acquisition of assets is transacted, any past tax liabilities associated with those assets carry forward with the acquirer in contrast to a purchase of stock where the same tax liabilities remain with the seller.

had a tenacious intellect and was one of the most creative dealmakers in the US. Henry and George didn't know Mike, but I believed once they became familiar with his accomplishments at ConAgra, they would want to do business with him.

Cliff and I agreed to proceed. Cliff would arrange an exclusive option[27] for ConAgra to evaluate the Beatrice tax issue. KKR would establish the valuation of the brands and familiarize George and Henry with ConAgra. Mike and his team found a way to live with the potential tax liability, and KKR was very impressed with ConAgra's business and Mike's acumen as a CEO. (In 1993, KKR named Mike CEO of RJR Nabisco after he retired from ConAgra.)

ConAgra acquired KKR's interest in Beatrice on June 7, 1990, almost exactly six months after I left Morgan Stanley. ConAgra paid $1.4 billion, half in cash and half in common and preferred stock. Gleacher & Company earned a $20 million fee. ConAgra's stock doubled over the next six months. KKR sold their position and made a most attractive exit from their Beatrice investment. I never again thought about the money I left behind at Morgan Stanley. Morale amongst the ten total employees at Gleacher was through the roof! Once again, I validated my long-held motto, "The world belongs to the aggressive."

---

27 An opportunity to evaluate a potential asset purchase or corporate acquisition without competition for an agreed period of time.

GLEACHER MORGAN GRENFELL

OUR FIRST YEAR IN BUSINESS WAS A RESOUNDING financial success. We created an international investment banking firm in partnership with a prominent UK merchant bank and the largest universal bank in Europe. I missed my friends at Morgan Stanley but what our new firm accomplished in its first year exceeded my expectations.

Gleacher Morgan Grenfell was busy over the next few years. Top partners Jim Goodwin, Jeff Tepper, Chas Phillips, Rob Engel, Conrad Meyer, Joe Donahue, Emil Henry, and Ken Ryan developed a continual stream of business with the firm's clients and contacts all over the world. Our partnership with Morgan Grenfell proved lucrative and professional. We sent people to work in London, and Morgan Grenfell sent people to New York. It started slowly, but after a few months, the senior banking partners in London realized we were a thoroughly professional organization and began to expose their clients to our partners in New York. Unsurprisingly, many of their UK and European clients were interested in the US market. Many assignments and much business evolved. Morgan Grenfell had been in business for many years and had built a client list characterized by "sticky" relationships. We were able to help them convert these clients into prospective and active US clients of the new firm even though in the past, almost all their business had been in the UK or Europe.

Deutsche was viewed in Germany as the ultimate commercial bank, but not as a sophisticated advisor capable of dealing with strategic situations either in their home market or North America. We were able to develop some business with large companies like Daimler Benz, which had very close ties with the bank, but it was tough slogging in Germany. My assumption that Deutsche would be a cash-generating partner did not pan out.

I realized prior to my first day at Lehman that I wanted to own equity in the firm where I worked. I did so at Lehman and at Morgan Stanley, and when I got up in the morning, it made a significant difference in how I felt about what I was doing. At Gleacher, the partners, including my assistant Marie Gentile, owned the equity, which made a difference in how they felt, how hard they worked, and how satisfied they were with their careers. Marie was able to send her two sons to MIT and Princeton, and both are extremely successful businessmen. As great as it was to work at a world-renowned firm like Morgan Stanley, owning equity in a small, highly respected firm transacting world-class business was even better.

Our deals in the late 1990s–early 2000s included American Home Products' $10 billion cash acquisition of American Cyanamid; the sale of MFS[28] to WorldCom for $14 billion; and the sale of Garantia in Brazil, the "Goldman Sachs" of South America, to Credit Suisse for $1.4 billion. We were the sole advisor on each transaction and owned an equity interest in MFS.

MFS

MFS was a subsidiary of the Peter Kiewit Company, a major construction firm based in Omaha, 100 percent owned by its employees. Walter Scott was Kiewit's CEO, and we met him through Mike Harper, who was the only nonemployee member of the Kiewit board of directors. Peter Kiewit owned pipelines and had decided to lay fiber-optic cable in the right of ways alongside the pipes.

Jim Goodwin did all the work on this project, and as with every situation in which Jim was involved, additional business followed. Jim majored in accounting in college, and

---

28 Metropolitan Fiber Systems is a telecommunications company with fiber-optic loops around major US and European cities.

when he graduated, he worked for a major accounting firm for a few years. He took the CPA exam, which in those days was administered only once a year. Jim got the highest score of the 50,000 people who took the exam that year! In the early days of our firm, Jim helped me immeasurably with the many challenges of starting a business from scratch. This task was complicated further by our rapid success and the amount of business each of us was responsible for. Jim was a superstar, and the clients he worked with knew it.

The MFS transaction was a major success for Kiewit and for us. We structured our engagement around warrants we received rather than a traditional cash success fee. This aligned our interests with those of Kiewit and provided more depth to the relationship than a one-time transaction fee would have. Our share of the $14 billion sale to WorldCom appreciated substantially. We sold our position well before Bernie Ebbers took WorldCom into bankruptcy and himself into federal prison for accounting fraud. Our engagement was an example of a creative structure possible in an independent firm which would not have been allowed in a major investment bank.

AMERICAN HOME PRODUCTS

Conrad Meyer did some of the heavy lifting on the Cyanamid deal. Conrad kept in touch with the corporate development staff at American Home Products and provided a window into what was going on at the company. I had a good relationship with Jack Stafford, the CEO. Conrad and I had been talking to our respective contacts about their interest in American Cyanamid, but nothing was progressing. One day in August 1994, a *Wall Street Journal* reporter called me looking for information. He told me Cyanamid was working on an asset-swap deal with another major company that he thought was close to getting done but was complex and moving slowly. He asked if I had heard anything about the Cyanamid transaction; I had not. It is not unusual for the press to look for information and, in this instance, it proved to be a stroke of good luck for American Home Products and us.

I called Jack Stafford, who was vacationing on Cape Cod. I related the *WSJ* phone call and said the asset-swap[29] deal must be nearing completion because the reporter was worried about losing his scoop if the deal happened without advance warning. Stafford told me he had spoken to Al Costello, the CEO of Cyanamid, a couple of days before and learned that he was taking a three-week golf trip to Ireland and would get in touch when he returned. I replied that not even the most avid golfers go on three-week golf trips to Ireland. One week, two weeks maybe—but not three. I told Jack I was sure Costello was stalling him until he could complete the asset deal and make it impossible for Jack to buy the

---

29 Two companies exchange business operations and/or equity, making a third-party acquisition of either difficult.

company. Jack asked me to meet him the next day at AHP's Madison, NJ headquarters.

Jack had the corporate helicopter pick him up early the following morning, and we sat down in a conference room at 9 a.m. Jack said he had spoken to the important members of his board, all of whom supported making a bid for Cyanamid. Conrad Meyer went through the valuation analysis and presented our recommendation that the bid should be $95 per Cyanamid share, a substantial premium over the current market price of around $60. The pharmaceutical industry was going through a consolidation phase, and we knew if our bid was too low other major companies would immediately turn up, Cyanamid would pick a white knight,[30] and we would end up with nothing. Jack never balked at our price recommendation and turned to the press release he would make when we announced the bid midday. The release went active, and both Cyanamid's and AHP's stocks immediately rose in market trading. The press reports were extremely positive, and two weeks later, the two CEOs turned the process into a "friendly" deal. The $9.7 billion acquisition was completed with $101 paid to each Cyanamid common share. Cyanamid's banker, Morgan Stanley, was unable to produce a white knight because the initial bid had anticipated the market correctly.

---

30 A company that outbids a hostile bidder and acquires a target company in a "friendly deal."

Other important deals in the 1994-1995 period included the sale of British Airways' 20 percent stake in US Air Group and the acquisition of General Electric's Kidder Peabody by Paine Webber. The night the Kidder Peabody deal was signed with GE, we had to resolve some loose ends. At about 2 a.m. I went to the GE building in Rockefeller Center to meet with Dennis Dammerman, GE's Chief Financial Officer. I entered a large conference room on the top floor, and much to my surprise, Dammerman was at a table with four other men. I knew Larry Bossidy, one of GE's top executives, and said, "Larry, what are you doing here?" He shrugged and replied, "Jack ordered us to stay here until the deal is done." The other three men and Larry were the four most senior operating executives responsible for managing GE's far-flung worldwide operations. The Kidder Peabody purchase had been one of the worst mistakes GE had made and was a major embarrassment for Jack Welch and his bullet-proof reputation. This deal was going to get done no matter what stood in the way. Dammerman and I easily sorted the remaining issues, and the deal was signed that night. I still get a chuckle thinking about Larry and the three other guys, summoned from all over the world, sitting there doing nothing at two o'clock in the morning.

After the Kidder Peabody transaction was put to bed, Jim Goodwin suggested we take a golf trip to Australia to celebrate the significant deals the firm had recently done. I had been to Australia when I was with Morgan Stanley to visit offices in Sydney and Melbourne. During that trip, Malcolm Turnbull and his wife, Lucy, gave a dinner party for me in Sydney. He later served as Prime Minister of Australia from 2015-2018, and Lucy was Lord Mayor of Sydney from 2002-2004, the first woman to serve in that capacity. I played Royal Melbourne with Cam Johnston, a solicitor who did work for Morgan Stanley. I was extremely impressed and placed the course in my global top five without question.

I liked Cam and his wife, Caroline, and we stayed in touch. Cam and the Secretary at Royal Melbourne arranged for five days of 36-hole golf for Jim and me on the many world-class golf courses in Melbourne. We had a fantastic week, and at the suggestion of John Craven, Chairman of Morgan Grenfell, I flew back with a stop in London to call on NatWest, Britain's second-largest bank. NatWest was in the press talking about expanding its investment banking business. John set up the meeting, and it went well, as they were curious about the recent Kidder deal with Paine Webber.

Soon after returning to New York, I received a call from NatWest. They had an opportunity to buy DLJ from Axa, a large French insurance company, and asked if our firm would represent them. DLJ, a successful investment bank, was a subsidiary of the Equitable Insurance Company in the US, which was a subsidiary of Axa. Our team worked on the valuation, and we recommended an offer of $2.5 billion. Axa was interested at that price, but DLJ management drew a line and said they wanted to go public and would leave if the company was sold to NatWest. Axa was not interested in escalating the matter, and it died. DLJ managed to go public and was eventually sold to Credit Suisse for $13 billion (later reputed to be the worst Wall Street acquisition ever).

Not long after the DLJ rejection, I received a call from Peter Hall, head of NatWest in North America. Peter asked if we would be interested in selling our business to NatWest. This was totally unsolicited and unexpected. I was noncommittal but told Peter I would think about the possibility. Jim Goodwin was the only person at the firm I consulted about the approach.

We were still in partnership with Deutsche and Morgan Grenfell at that time, but the situation had begun to change. The partnership had been ongoing for five and a half years, and although its results were good, Deutsche had expanded its horizon and decided it was time to ramp up its global advisory business under the Deutsche brand. Deutsche told me they wanted to buy Gleacher and have us spearhead their expansion. I spoke to John Craven, who had been a member of Deutsche's Vorstand, or board of directors, for six years and told him I was not inclined to become part of the bank. He confided he was also working toward disengaging as he found the culture and bureaucracy stifling. He was the only non-German on the Vorstand.

Jim Goodwin and I worked on a valuation and concluded if we got a price of $135 million for our business we would have done well for the partners. We decided not to go forward with Deutsche, so it made sense to have a serious discussion with NatWest.

We received two other unsolicited offers at virtually the same time! Swiss Bank Corporation had recently acquired S. G. Warburg in London, the leading investment bank in Europe, and wanted to expand globally. We would become the North American piece of the puzzle with the Swiss instead of the Germans and with Warburg, which would be a stronger European partner than Morgan Grenfell. I had dinner with the CEO in London, and he reminded me of the Deutsche Bank people. I happened to notice a ring of about ten to fifteen keys attached to a belt loop on his suit trousers and that also threw me off. I thought it strange a CEO of a major international bank would attach a key ring to the pants of his bespoke suit. I decided I would let this potential opportunity pass.

Last but not least, I received a call from Bill Harrison, CEO of JPMorgan. He told me the bank had lots of business opportunities but lacked someone to lead the major deals. He said Jack Stafford, a long-time JPM board member, told him I was the best person he could think of to lead that effort. Bill Harrison is an outstanding person and executive, universally admired by the business community and people in general, including me. We had a good meeting (we played golf), and I told Bill we had a variety of options for our business and had not yet decided on one. I knew Gleacher's partners would strengthen JPM's M&A team, but I worried a deal with JPM would be too much like returning to Morgan Stanley. Bill and I never took matters further, as he called a few days later and told me Jimmy Lee, a senior colleague, was opposed and thought they didn't need to buy a firm but could enhance their M&A operation on their own. I am sure Jimmy also felt he did not need competition from a new senior team member at the bank. I did not disagree with Jimmy's instincts one bit! He and I were friendly, and many people, myself included, were saddened by his unexpected death years later.

The combination of the various discussions with Deutsche, Swiss Bank Corp, JPMorgan, and NatWest made our decision obvious. If we could negotiate the price we wanted from NatWest and get their agreement to provide the capital required to build a high-yield debt business and leverage finance capability, we could create a firm comparable to DLJ since we already had a superior M&A business.

NatWest agreed to our valuation and plan, and the firm was named Gleacher NatWest. We chose NatWest common stock worth $135 million as payment because we believed their stock was undervalued. They were happy to pay in cash, loan notes, whatever currency we wanted. I would guess not many sellers would have chosen 100 percent common stock as payment for their business, but to Jim Goodwin and me, it was a no-brainer. At that time, NatWest common traded at around £6 on the London Stock Exchange. I sold mine for just under £19 a few years later, as did most of Gleacher's partners.

The new arrangement thrived for the next few years. The high-yield business we established was very profitable, and we created a mezzanine investment fund[31] run by an excellent partner named Elliot Jones. Under Elliot's management, the fund became a major success. Our arrangement with NatWest included a split of pre-tax income, 58 percent to Gleacher and 42 percent to NatWest. This enabled us to build the business and compensate our people well. The original partners of Gleacher were making more cash than before the sale and had their share of the sale proceeds to boot. Morale was high!

Some good things eventually end. After our deal, NatWest hired the head of Morgan Stanley's equity derivatives team to run their global equity business. NatWest asked me to check this person out at Morgan Stanley, and the feedback I got was negative. I passed this on to NatWest, but they hired him anyway. The derivatives operation and Gleacher NatWest's business did not overlap. Within a couple of years, a large derivatives position evolved into a major unrealized

---

31 A pool of capital invested in subordinated debt and equity securities in leveraged
   finance buyouts and private equity investments.

loss that had not yet been discovered by NatWest's top management. Since the loss was unrealized, it was not required to be reported in the bank's financial statements. We got wind of what was happening and spoke to management. We were concerned the potential loss might be so large it would affect the solvency of the bank and the value of our common stock holdings. This caused top management to implement drastic changes.

Management knew if they wrote off the positions and disclosed the damage, they would be terminated. The UK press was skeptical about the big British clearing banks' investment banking initiatives, and a surprise major trading loss would cause a firestorm of negative publicity. Management's solution was to announce the bank's exit from investment banking and bury the derivatives' loss in the many write-offs the exit would require.

This tactic worked for management, and no senior officials were dismissed, but it caused Gleacher to make a coursecorrection. We had negotiated a "no change of control clause" in our sale agreement with the bank. This meant if NatWest wanted to sell our business, we had the right to buy it back for book value, which we did. We paid the bank about $4 million (the value of the furnishings, computers, etc.) and took over the lease of our office from which we had never moved. The Bank of Scotland provided a $500 million line of credit to enable us to continue trading and underwriting high-yield debt. We used very little of the line as the high-yield market was weak and getting weaker and we exited the high-yield business within a year of buying the company back.

MANAGEMENT STYLE

———

AS A MANAGER, I WAS GENERALLY REPUTED TO BE tough. That can be attributed partly to my aura as a former Marine and partly to my inability to suffer fools. I had the highest of standards, and those who failed to rise to them didn't last very long. All that said, I am absolutely certain a random sample of the large number of professionals who worked for me during my forty-five-year career would say I was fair and honest and pulled no punches—they always knew where they stood with me.

The table of organization in an M&A operation within a major firm or boutique investment bank is flat. The head of M&A is responsible for a horizontal line of partners who transact the deals. I met or spoke with each partner every week and discussed the most important deals he or she was working on to make sure partners were not wasting their time on low-odds situations or making questionable tactical assumptions, but it was up to them make the situation work for the client without more handholding from above.

There simply wasn't time for it. This approach made each partner more confident and stronger, and most of the time, each found a way to succeed.

My style of motivating and teaching young people was to lead by example, and as I had learned in the Marines, to never ask anyone to do something I could not do myself. There was a cost associated with this level of commitment. Family vacations were disrupted and my children's sporting and school events were often missed. At times it was difficult, but people watch the leader's every move and listen to every word the leader speaks. When I worked on the major deals described in this book, every eye was watching—the global business world, the press, all the competitors, and every person at my firm and at the company we were representing. The young people were motivated by the success our hard work delivered, and this made them proud to be members of our team.

Another tenet of leadership I learned from my experience in the Marines was to push forward the most promising talent by putting them in charge of important initiatives that would challenge them and enhance confidence when conducted successfully. I was at a large gathering two years ago and met up with Bill Ford, CEO of the $34 billion growth equity firm General Atlantic, whom I had not seen in a long time. We said hello, and he immediately reminded me of the sale of a subsidiary for Warner-Lambert, of which I put him in charge when we were at Morgan Stanley. Bill was a young Vice President and this was a deal for an important client, which normally would be staffed with a partner in charge. He said he was really nervous at the outset, but after he succeeded, his self-confidence and motivation were at all-time highs. He thanked me for doing the single best thing anyone had ever done for him in the advancement of his career.

Sometimes being a good manager meant not worrying about winning popularity contests. One example of maintaining high standards involved Matt Denison, a personal favorite of mine when he was a young associate at Gleacher & Company. Nathaniel Rothschild, a former Gleacher analyst who had risen to success and acclaim as a global investor and entrepreneur, came to us seeking advice about a business problem. Nat owned a minority interest in a public company that had significant issues. He was trying to decide whether to buy control and clean up the company or sell his stock and get out. He asked us for a recommendation. We agreed to study the situation and get back to Nat in a week. I asked Matt Denison to do the analytical work and share his preliminary thoughts with me. He returned in a few days with a rather thick book of quantitative analyses that offered no thoughts or conclusions. Matt, at that stage of his career, was comfortable doing the numbers but was reticent to communicate what he thought they indicated. I tossed the book into my trash basket without even a cursory glance and told Matt to come back and give me the advice he would give to our client and not to worry about being right or wrong. I wish I had a picture of the look on his face! He came back the next day, and we discussed our options and agreed our advice would be to sell the existing minority interest and exit the situation. Matt told me recently, not the first time he's done so, the lesson he learned then has been the most valuable of his career. It taught him what he must do to succeed. Matt is now a director at Madison Dearborn Partners, a major private equity firm. Nat Rothschild agreed with our advice and liquidated his position.

GLEACHER & CO 2.0

ASSET MANAGEMENT

Emil Henry was a Gleacher partner for over ten years. He was intent on creating an investment arm for the firm. Emil was the driving force behind the money raised for our $300 million mezzanine fund, which returned 30 percent gross. All the partners were invested in the fund and also received 50 percent of the carried interest. The 2d mezz fund raised $500 million, and again, we achieved superior results. Our success would not have happened without Emil. He also spent a year raising a $125 million private equity fund. Others in the firm helped, but again, without Emil, it wouldn't have happened. It was not easy for an M&A firm to raise a "first" private equity fund in 1995.

The fund closed on $125 million, almost exactly when we negotiated the sale of Gleacher to NatWest. Our lawyers advised it would take nine months to a year to try to obtain Fed approval to conduct both M&A advisory business and principal investing activities in a firm owned by a commercial bank. They said we would most likely gain approval, but it was not 100 percent certain. It became clear we could not do both—we should either sell to NatWest or become a private equity firm. We sold for $135 million, a decision based on "bird in the hand" reasoning. In retrospect, the better decision might have been the private equity route given the rapid growth of that business since the mid-nineties, but at the time, we made the right call.

WEBMD

We made many venture capital investments over the years at Gleacher. Our reputation as advisors and venture investors attracted entrepreneurs. One day we met twenty-seven-year-old Jeff Arnold from Atlanta. Jeff had already sold his first company for a serious amount of money and had formed a new company called WebMD. Jeff was as good a salesperson as I had ever met, and I liked the business plan of WebMD. The company was tiny, but it was not difficult to see its potential. I invested $1 million and eventually joined the board. Jeff developed the company at warp speed, making an acquisition almost every week. We got to the point where a registration statement was being prepared, and WebMD was planning on going public. Right at that point, we were approached by Healtheon, a public company founded by Jim Clark, who also founded Netscape, and John Doerr of Kleiner Perkins, the legendary Silicon Valley venture capital firm. Healtheon was a perfect fit with WebMD and was already public. Clark and Doerr were icons of the internet and VC[32] investing because Netscape had opened access to the internet for the world. Merging Healtheon and WebMD was a no-brainer if the terms were right. That was my job.

We met in a hotel conference room in Atlanta. Clark and Doerr had come from California because Healtheon was pursuing WebMD. I remember Doerr unpacking a bag he carried that contained nothing but tangled wires. I assumed he carried numerous devices that required power, some of which, perhaps, had not yet been made available to the public. One could regard this display as either humorous or a sly show of force!

Healtheon was trading at a price that reflected the aura of Clark and Doerr more than an economic appraisal of its modest earnings and cash flow. WebMD was in approximately the same economic position but obviously had not yet benefited from the validation and excitement it undoubtedly would create in the public market. One of the small, West Coast boutiques who worked with tech companies had sent a young associate to accompany Clark and Doerr. I was surprised when he started talking about the relative values of the two companies without being asked. I was further surprised at the gibberish coming out of his

---

32 Venture capital: the riskiest form of equity investment, which is made in young or startup companies.

mouth. He was talking about the coefficient of this and the coefficient of that, implying that whatever he was trying to say multiplied the value of Healtheon relative to WebMD. I had enough. I said, "Stop! Nothing you are saying makes any sense. I've never heard, nor do I understand what your theory is supposed to be. These companies are similar, and both have great potential. One is public, and if people want, we can wait until WebMD has gone public and compare the relative valuations. If there is a deal to be done here today, it's going to be a 50:50 merger of equals."

After thirty seconds of awkward silence, a more rational business discussion ensued, rather than propeller-head talk. Eventually, we agreed on a 50:50 deal. Clark and Doerr wisely wanted to get something done to create momentum and excitement in the market for their investment. They realized the fit with WebMD was uniquely strong and did not want to forego the opportunity. They definitely did not want to roll the dice and see which stock traded higher once WebMD went public.

After the merger, the combined company was named WebMD and its stock traded as high as $127 a share, up from a starting price of around $20. After a couple of years, Jeff Arnold departed for his next startup, and WebMD plodded forward. Its lofty valuation didn't stick, but it still exists today and provides valuable healthcare information to the public worldwide.

GARANTIA

One morning in 1998, Claudio Haddad called my office in New York. Marie screened my calls, and I did not know Claudio Haddad, so I did not respond. He called back a few minutes later and explained to Marie that he was the managing partner of Garantia, a Brazilian investment bank located in Sao Paulo. He went on to say he had a PhD in economics from The University of Chicago and had attended a World Economic Forum event at the Gleacher Center. I took the call.

Garantia, which neither my partner Jeff Tepper nor I had heard of, turned out to be a highly successful firm, known widely in the southern hemisphere as the "Goldman Sachs of South America." The firm transacted corporate finance and M&A business but was primarily a fixed-income trading platform. There were nineteen partners, half in their fifties and sixties, half in their thirties. Two years earlier, Garantia had made a profit of almost $1 billion but had suffered serious trading losses in the most recent year. Claudio told me the older group had the majority of the votes and wanted to sell the firm to protect their capital from further trading losses. Jeff and I spent a few days in Sao Paulo meeting Claudio and Jorge Paulo Lemann, the senior partner, getting familiar with the business and the firm's culture. We then conducted an international process that identified Goldman Sachs and Credit Suisse as the most interested potential acquirers. Credit Suisse won the day and paid $1.4 billion for Garantia. I was most appreciative Claudio decided to call back!

SANDLER O'NEILL

Jimmy Dunne and I became friends through our mutual interest in golf. Jimmy was head of trading at Sandler O'Neill, and through him, I became acquainted with Herman Sandler and Chris Quackenbush. Sandler O'Neill had carved out a niche working with medium-sized commercial banks who flew under the radar of major investment banks focused on larger opportunities. Sandler offered sales, trading, and investment banking to its clients and was consistently profitable. Chris was head of investment banking, and Herman Sandler was the senior partner.

Late in the afternoon of September 10, 2001, Chris and I were on the phone putting the finishing touches on a document we planned to use to offer a 25 percent equity interest in Sandler to a carefully selected list of European banks. We decided to meet in Sandler's office at the World Trade Center to finalize the offering memorandum. I couldn't do it the following morning because I had a meeting in New Jersey, so Chris and I agreed to meet first thing Wednesday.

Tragically, more than half of the 300 employees of Sandler died in the World Trade Center, including Chris Quackenbush and Herman Sandler. Jimmy Dunne survived as he was out of the office trying to qualify for the USGA Mid-Amateur Championship. Jimmy, almost single-handedly, persevered through the immense pain and trauma and rebuilt Sandler O'Neill into an even stronger entity than before. The Sandler investment banking group operated from excess space in Gleacher's offices for nine months until they moved into new Sandler space in mid-town Manhattan. The survival and successful reemergence of Sandler is one of the most uplifting and impressive post-9/11 achievements.

AIG

In 2008, the massive insurer AIG[33] was nearly bankrupted by billions of dollars of credit default swaps gone bad in the financial crisis. The US government decided the damage of an AIG bankruptcy would be potentially catastrophic and injected $85 billion of equity in an attempt to salvage the company. We were told AIG was interviewing bankers to sell expendable assets and further reinforce the company's chances for survival. Hank Greenberg, AIG's legendary Chairman and CEO, had been relieved and separated from the company. Mickey Cohen, an independent member of its board and a partner at a law firm in Toronto, was managing all transactions.

I called Mickey, who said he was familiar with my career but I was late to the party. He said he had "pretty much decided" who he was going to hire and was reluctant to invite me to come to Toronto for no reason. Once again, I used the "my

---

33 American International Group operates in multinational finance and insurance in eighty countries.

nickel" argument. He said, "Well, on that basis, I'd like to meet you."

Ken Ryan and I flew to Toronto and joined Mickey at his office the following day. Mickey was bright, affable, and relaxed. We had a vigorous discussion of AIG and its derivatives operations. We told Mickey how much major transaction experience Ken and I had accumulated, which made us well-positioned to clear his path to success. We promised that, if hired, Ken and I would do all the work. He said, "Let's go have lunch." We did, and we went home that afternoon with the assignment.

When the AIG assignment was finished—and by the way, the Treasury made a $23 billion profit from the sale of their equity stake—Mickey joined the Gleacher board and was far and away, the most capable and helpful director. We remain good friends. So much for taking no for an answer!

BANK OF SCOTLAND

About six months after we bought our business back from NatWest I received a call from Peter Burt. He told me he and his board had concluded the Bank of Scotland was too small to compete at the highest level of commercial banking. BOS made significant profit from leveraged lending and was widely recognized in the UK as the top practitioner in that field. Peter realized his balance sheet was too small now that competition had increased with the major clearing banks in London, who were eager to get more involved in this highly profitable business. He asked if I was in a position to help BOS evaluate a bid for NatWest, who had recently announced a merger with Legal & General, a dull UK insurance company. The Legal & General merger proposal, with L&G management taking control of NatWest, was received poorly by the British press and stock market. I was the largest noninstitutional stockholder in NatWest but had no privileged or "inside information." Some people criticized my participation, but I paid no attention since I no longer was an employee of NatWest and was free to do whatever I wished. I told Peter I would relish the opportunity to work with him and his board, and NatWest was sorely in need of a solution to their current malaise.

I had known Peter Burt for twenty years. We met at Muirfield, the famous Scottish golf club, in 1979. Our mutual friend Gene Goodwillie, an American lawyer and a life-long friend of mine, arranged a golf game and invited Peter, a low handicap player, to take part. Peter and I had much in common. He received an MBA from Wharton and was working his way up at the BOS, and I had an MBA from Chicago and was a young partner at Lehman. Our golf skills matched up perfectly—we played each other for the next thirty-five years at scratch, no strokes—and over the years, the results were probably close to a draw. Our families became friendly, and we spent many holidays together. It was an extremely special relationship.

NatWest was in a weakened state due to the unpopularity of the pending Legal & General merger. The uncertainty around whether shareholders would approve such a questionable deal, if it ever came to the required vote, also loomed over the situation. A BOS bid would create a lot of interest, but two countervailing factors required consideration. NatWest was five times the size of BOS, and it was certain the Royal Bank of Scotland, also based in Edinburgh, would compete. RBS was slightly larger than BOS and was also a respected competitor in the UK market. We didn't think the size factor would derail a BOS bid because NatWest was in such a weak position, and its size precluded another of the big UK clearing banks from bidding due to anticompetitive retail banking regulations. We didn't think non-UK banks would be interested. However, the likely counterbid from RBS would clearly be a formidable challenge. Peter and his board concluded they had a unique opportunity to make a bold initiative and possibly win. They decided to make the bid at a board meeting in Edinburgh and set up an analysts' meeting in London the following day. Shortly before 9 a.m. the next morning, the cavernous room in the city[34] was packed. Jeff Tepper, Chas Phillips, and I were there.

Peter announced the bid, and the crowd erupted in yells and applause. I'd never seen anything like it in business. NatWest stock jumped 40 percent at the opening of the market, and BOS stock also traded up all day. The press

34 London's financial district, equivalent to New York's Wall Street.

unanimously concluded this was the best thing that could happen to NatWest, and Peter was anointed the commercial banker of his generation in the UK. Peter met with analysts and the press for the remainder of the day, and Jeff, Chas, and I went to my club in London for a workout and lunch before flying back to New York. We celebrated, but we knew a difficult struggle with RBS was coming. Nonetheless, it was one of the most exciting and unforgettable days of my business career.

As expected, RBS made a counterbid, and the process of each bank trying to persuade the big UK investment institutions to support its offer carried on for months. There was an ebb and flow to this dance: one week, things would look promising, and the next, the tide would go out. Ultimately, the major institutional shareholders supported RBS, probably because they were slightly larger than BOS and were thought to have greater depth of management. It was obviously a major disappointment for Peter and his board, and for me. Later on, the decision would prove devastating for the institutions and their clients.

During the first few years after taking control of NatWest, RBS focused on cutting costs. They fired most of the senior management and related staff, except those in retail banking, where NatWest was popular and profitable, particularly in England. RBS kept the brass NatWest nameplates of the retail bank in all the branches, so to the customers, NatWest was still NatWest. The name of the combined banks was changed to RBS. As the savings rolled in, RBS became one of the five best-performing stocks in the world. The value of my former NatWest shares (now RBS) more than tripled, but as the savings began to decrease, hubris reared its ugly head.

Fred Goodwin, CEO of RBS, orchestrated a $98.5 billion acquisition of ABN AMRO,[35] the Dutch commercial bank. I immediately sold my stock because I believed the deal was too large for RBS to manage and my regard for Fred Goodwin had become quite negative as I got to know him after the NatWest deal. The ABN acquisition became a disaster, and RBS was nationalized. In due course, Fred "The Shred" Goodwin was fired, his knighthood was rescinded, and his pension was cut in half. The British government nationalized the bank, investing £42 billion to avert bankruptcy. RBS stock has since traded as low as 19 pence, creating a paper loss of £26 billion for the government's investment. The name of the bank was recently changed from RBS to NatWest and the government still owns 62.4 percent of the shares. Too bad Peter didn't win. This debacle would never have happened if he had. Bad luck for the pensioners whose retirement money was managed by the institutions that supported RBS.

Gleacher sold BOS to Halifax, a major mortgage bank, and Peter retired. He was knighted and became Chairman of

---

35 Algemene Bank Nederland–Amsterdam Rotterdam Bank was acquired by the Royal Bank of Scotland in 2012 for $98.5 billion.

Gleacher Partners in London, a director of Shell Oil and chairman of a number of British companies.

During the 2000s, as a steady flow of M&A business continued, we opened offices in Chicago and Atlanta; entered the hedge funds business; created a successful restructuring operation; made many venture capital investments; formed Gleacher Shacklock in London with Tim Shacklock, a highly regarded senior investment banker; and came into 2008 with a full book of M&A business.

The financial crisis of 2008 did enormous worldwide damage to many businesses. Lehman went bankrupt and disappeared. Merrill Lynch would have done the same had Bank of America not acquired them at the eleventh hour. Goldman Sachs, Morgan Stanley, and all the big commercial banks received government bailout funding and survived. All of our M&A deals fell apart with the exception of General Dynamics' $2.2 billion purchase of Jet Aviation, a German company owned by Permira, a major private equity firm based in London. Ken Ryan represented GD and miraculously closed the deal on October 2, two weeks after the Lehman bankruptcy. It was helpful Tom Lister had become CEO of Permira. Tom had worked with me years before at Morgan Stanley, and Ken had worked with him when Forstmann Little, at which Tom was a partner, acquired IMG.

ONE THAT GOT AWAY

THE FIFTEEN-YEAR LEASE ON OUR OFFICES IN NEW York was up for renewal at the end of 2008, and I decided at age sixty-eight, I wasn't interested in signing on the dotted line for another fifteen years! I told our guys many times I would never be an old man coming into the office every morning.

For some time, a publicly-traded company named Broadpoint had been pursuing us. Broadpoint had high-yield and mortgage-backed securities sales and trading components and aspired to add investment banking. Sales and trading businesses are completely different from investment banking, and the types of people involved in each differ just as much. Traders and bond salesmen and investment bankers usually don't mix well, making them hard to manage under one roof. Nevertheless, in the gloom of the late 2008 environment, Gleacher agreed to be acquired by Broadpoint for $180 million in cash and common stock. The new company created a fair amount of interest early on, and we raised

$160 million in cash in a public offering of common stock managed by Merrill Lynch. Our stock market value was in excess of a billion dollars.

After a year or so, the outside directors became uncomfortable with the CEO and forced him to resign. A candidate for the job had run the asset management business at Deutsche Bank and had worked in mortgage finance at Merrill Lynch, which seemed to dovetail advantageously with our mortgage operation. He talked a good game, and the other directors and I were unanimously in favor of hiring him.

Unfortunately, it quickly became clear our new CEO had no idea how to develop the business of our firm. He failed to earn the respect of many senior employees and made changes to our mortgage business, which resulted in serious financial problems for the company. The other senior people and I realized the situation was serious, even though we had $180 million of cash and no debt.

I found a solution that would successfully resolve the situation for all concerned, including the public shareholders. Ron Kruszewski, the CEO of Stifel, a leading regional securities firm based in St. Louis, MO, had indicated six months earlier he'd like to discuss the possibility of acquiring the merged company, so I got word to Ron to call if he was still interested. Ron called immediately, and we met at my house in New York City the following morning.

Stifel had recently made a number of acquisitions, the largest being Keefe, Bruyette & Woods, a bank specialist firm similar to Sandler O'Neill, which Stifel had acquired for $550 million. I explained Gleacher had around $180 million of cash and no debt, and the high-yield business was doing well, but mortgage trading was mired in problems of its own creation. Investment banking was profitable and currently involved in a number of large M&A deals, including one I was working on that would settle out at around $20 billion. Ron said he wanted to make a deal. He was very interested in the high-yield group, didn't want to count out the mortgage business, and wanted me to work with him to help build Stifel into a larger and stronger entity. He sent a letter to our board members offering $250 million subject to due diligence and an acceptable arrangement with a majority of the high-yield salesmen and traders. I was not enthusiastic about going to work for Stifel but liked Ron and admired his aggressiveness in building up his firm. A deal with Stifel would rescue our firm from a much worse fate that I was sure would otherwise develop.

We had a board meeting the next morning. One of the directors brought a lawyer who advised the board to form a special committee to deal with the Stifel offer. I countered that the company was going to disintegrate if we did not do this deal. I asserted the CEO and the three assistants he had hired were not equipped to manage and build the business for many reasons, including their absurd plan to hire 150 additional investment bankers and their bad decisions that had caused serious problems in the mortgage business. Furthermore, a private equity investor with three board seats and I collectively owned 40 percent of the firm, and we wanted to sell, not buy the company. A special committee was not required to evaluate the possible sale; it was necessary only if management was trying to acquire a company they were managing (for the shareholders). The board member's lawyer asserted a special committee was required to reduce the personal liability of all the board members since a very large percentage of the board had already decided to sell. Given that advice, the majority of the board decided to form a special committee.

I thought this was an absurd legal tactic. In retrospect, I should have resigned on the spot, made public the conditional offer from Stifel, and allowed the chips to fall as they may. The stock would have risen sharply, and the board's liability would have increased if, as I had predicted, it did nothing, and the company showed signs of failure. I decided not to resign because I thought I would have a greater impact on the situation as Chairman of the Board than I could on the outside. Also, I wanted to close the $20 billion M&A deal I had been working on. I didn't want to leave my client in a lurch and sacrifice a $20 million fee for the firm.

The CEO was put in charge of the sale process, and he and the board member who'd brought his lawyer joined forces and never allowed Stifel to talk to the high-yield personnel. The CEO and his team provided the board with "fantasy" projections that valued the firm at approximately $400 million. They dragged things out with meaningless meetings with other "potential" bidders, which never came close to amounting to anything. There are many provocative theories about what the board member and the CEO were trying to accomplish with their tactics. The inevitable result was the CEO losing a $10 million payment he would have received had the firm been sold, and the public shareholders being denied an opportunity to receive an attractive price for their shares. I closed the $20 billion M&A deal at the end of 2012 and resigned.

Within a few months of my resignation, most members of the high-yield group were hired surreptitiously by Baird, a regional investment firm, and walked out of their office in New Jersey one day, never to return. They surely could have done a similar deal with Stifel, a firm more highly regarded than Baird. The CEO and his team were completely blindsided. Shortly after the high-yield defection, the troubled mortgage group also left en masse and joined an obscure firm. The board fired the CEO and was forced to liquidate the business. Almost $100 million in cash was distributed to the shareholders.

The directors had failed to grasp the obvious, and the firm disintegrated in slow motion right before their eyes.

LOOKING FORWARD

I'VE HAD THE PRIVILEGE OF SPEAKING TO MANY groups of young people and teaching classes at all the top business schools. Whenever I do so, the venue is filled with men and women who want to know what it takes to succeed. I tell them that leadership skills, willingness to take chances, and finding the will to win are the characteristics that enabled me to succeed in business and in life. I talk about the many CEOs from around the world who told me what they valued most was their certainty my advice was unaffected by outside influence. My reliance on flawless integrity, instilled in me during my service in the Marine Corps, had served me well. CEOs also had high regard for my ability to concisely simplify complex advice to their boards, which almost always led the directors to approve the course of action the CEO and I were advocating.

Western Illinois, Northwestern, and The University of Chicago played important roles in my personal development, and I wanted them to share my success. My friend, Chas

Phillips, told me philanthropy would be a more significant dimension of my life than financial gain. As usual, he was right, but of course, one doesn't happen without the other.

I take great pride in the two Gleacher Golf Centers built twenty-three years apart at Northwestern, the Gleacher Center campus and the Veterans Scholarship Fund at Chicago Booth, and the golf course built at Western Illinois named for Harry Mussatto. In 1995, the $15 million I donated to The University of Chicago was matched by alumni contributions, thus financing the new Gleacher Center Business School campus off North Michigan Avenue on the Chicago River. A few years ago, prompted by my opinion that veterans are underappreciated in this country, I founded a Veterans Scholarship Fund with a $10 million contribution for Booth veterans, raised another $10 million from Mike Harper's family foundation, and named the fund in Mike's honor. The $20-million fund is unique among major business schools and has attracted many outstanding individuals to Booth. There are close to 100 veterans at Booth at present, and the school wants to increase that number. Veterans add a valuable dynamic to the classes and teams. Most of the veterans at Booth were officers and had served in leadership positions during their active duty. This valuable experience, combined with a Chicago MBA, will position some to become leaders in our economy as CEOs, entrepreneurs, and government officials who will contribute to our country's economic success.

I sincerely appreciate the gratitude I received over the years from male and female golfers from all over the world who decided to attend Northwestern partially because of the outstanding golf training facilities, from veterans who were able to secure a Chicago MBA with the financial support of the scholarship fund I created, and from many people at Western Illinois who benefit from having an 18-hole golf course adjacent to the campus.

I hope this book will encourage readers to take risks, reward those who helped on the way to success, and then repeat the process by paying it forward and motivating the next generation to do the same.

One final suggestion: always remember, the world belongs to the aggressive!

ACKNOWLEDGMENTS

———

THANK YOU, STEVE GILBERT, FOR GIVING ME THE direction to get started with the process of writing this book. Steve suggested once I got into it, I would be amazed at how much I would remember, and I would enjoy the creative stimulation. He was right about both, as he is about almost everything.

Thank you, Marie Gentile, my invaluable assistant and friend for the past thirty-two years, for putting the very earliest drafts of the manuscript in good order while providing your usual encouragement and good judgement about how to carry on with the project.

Thank you, Ellen Katz, for reading an early draft of the manuscript and making some useful suggestions, which I incorporated. Ellen worked at Harvard Business School on a Written Analysis of Cases (WAC) course back in the day.

Most of all, thank you, Jimmy Gleacher (my son), for working often and diligently as my partner in creating this book. Jimmy taught me how to edit and use the relevant tools on my laptop. I couldn't have unlocked either on my own. Jimmy has written four published books and the screenplay for a movie. He is a professional. He did not affect my voice while providing indispensable organizational and editorial improvements to the manuscript.

Best of all, Jimmy and I worked hard and efficiently as a team and enjoyed every minute of our collaboration. One day, we worked for fourteen hours. Our successful teamwork also found its way to the golf course. In the old days, Jimmy would announce that it "pissed him off" whenever I'd offer advice about his golf technique. Now, once in a while, when we play, Jimmy asks me to give him a lesson! Small things in life are often the most rewarding. Thanks, Jimmy, for being such a wonderful son.

ABOUT THE AUTHOR

———

ERIC GLEACHER founded the M&A business at Lehman Brothers, ran the Global M&A operation at Morgan Stanley, and founded one of the first successful M&A boutiques, which he managed for twenty-three years. He is widely recognized as one of a handful of investors and financiers who launched M&A into the global industry it is today.

Gleacher was a US Marine infantry officer in the '60s and is a graduate of Northwestern University and The University of Chicago. An only child, he now has six children, a stepson and stepdaughter, and eight grandchildren. He is married to Paula Gleacher, an artist and avid golfer.

INDEX

A

Agee, Bill, 137, 138, 139, 141
Allied Corporation, 136, 137, 138, 139, 140, 141
American Cyanamid Company, 195, 196, 197, 198
American Home Products Corporation, 195, 196, 197
American National Bank, 43, 44
Anderson, Warren, 167
Arnold, Jeff, 212, 214
AT&T Corporation, 69, 71, 173, 174
AXA Group, 200, 201

B

Ball, George W, 111, 127, 128
Bandon Dunes, 77, 78, 79
Bank of America, 223
Bank of Scotland, 205, 218, 220
Barkow, Al, 38
Beatrice Foods Co., 191, 192
Beck, Jeff, 180, 182
Bendix Corporation, 136, 137, 138, 139, 140
Bergerac, Michel, 161, 162, 163, 164
Bershad, Steve, 132
Bienen, Henry, 66
Black, Bill, 146, 149, 151, 155
Black, Leon, 166, 180